Wkeman

5·9·83.

Daddy,
with all my love,
Happy Birthday
- Kay.
x

GW00759303

CAPTAIN'S INNINGS

CAPTAIN'S INNINGS

An Autobiography

Keith Fletcher

Stanley Paul
London Melbourne Sydney Auckland Johannesburg

Stanley Paul & Co. Ltd

An imprint of the Hutchinson Publishing Group

17–21 Conway Street, London W1P 6JD

Hutchinson Group (Australia) Pty Ltd
30–32 Cremorne Street, Richmond South, Victoria 3121
PO Box 151, Broadway, New South Wales 2007

Hutchinson Group (NZ) Ltd
32–34 View Road, PO Box 40-086, Glenfield, Auckland 10

Hutchinson Group (SA) Pty Ltd
PO Box 337, Bergvlei 2012, South Africa

First published 1983
© Keith Fletcher 1983

Set in Linotron Baskerville by Input Typesetting Ltd, London

Printed in Great Britain by Anchor Press Ltd
and bound by Wm Brendon & Son Ltd
both of Tiptree, Essex

British Library Cataloguing in Publication Data
Fletcher, Keith
   Captain's innings.
   1. Fletcher, Keith   2. Cricket players–
   Great Britain–Biography
   I. Title   II. Lee, Alan
   796.35′8′0924   GV915.F/

ISBN 0 09 152410 5

Contents

PHOTOGRAPHIC ACKNOWLEDGEMENTS

For permission to reproduce photographs included in this book, the publisher and author would like to thank Central Press Photos Ltd, *Daily Star*, Express & Independent Newspapers Ltd of Leytonstone, Michael Johnson, Lawrence Lustig, Adrian Murrell, All-Sport and Sport and General Press Agency Ltd.

1

The Caldecote Cowfield

Tin Town lies just outside Cambridge, off the main road to St Neots. To a young lad growing up soon after the last war, it seemed the most important place in the world. Now, as I look back, it is a village still filled with good memories and good people, some of the friendliest I have ever known.

For the unitiated majority, Tin Town was the local nickname for the village of Caldecote. In those days of rehabilitation for the country, our village contained more than its share of houses made largely of tin, and the phrase stuck with the place for a number of years.

The Fletcher family, mother and father, my elder brother Barry and myself, had moved into the village – and a brick house – in 1948. The previous four years of my life had been spent in Worcester, which puzzles a lot of people, especially when they hear the distinct south London accent of my Dad. There was a simple reason for it. My parents both originated from the Peckham and Camberwell area of the capital, but when life there became precarious during the war, they were evacuated to Worcester. Barry was born in 1940 and I arrived four years later, but neither of us reflects on Worcester as being home. Barry still lives and works in Caldecote now, and I think of it as the scene of a very happy childhood.

School, however, never featured high among my list of priorities. It was something to be tolerated, enjoyable only when it involved playing sport – which was never often enough for my liking.

The village school at Caldecote catered only for infants,

and when I graduated from there I was sent to Bourne, the next village but a bus ride away. Our school bus rarely ran reliably to time but my friends and I looked forward to the mornings when it was late. If nine o'clock came and the bus had still not arrived, we took it upon ourselves to declare school finished for the day, and went home. This happened quite often, so perhaps it was not surprising that I did not emerge among the brightest pupils in Cambridgeshire.

Academically, I was hopeless. At the time, it never seemed to matter. I knew I was not very clever and, if I am honest, I did little to improve things. There were 120 senior pupils at our school, and only two teachers, one of whom took me for every lesson from maths to religious instruction. He must have come to despair of little Fletcher, who neither showed any interest in his work nor put any effort into it. Now, of course, I wish I had worked harder and maybe even obtained some qualifications, but passing examinations was a remote and unattractive thought when I actually had the chance. From a very early age, my thoughts were directed far more towards a different sort of test – with a capital T.

My father had begun to play cricket for Caldecote soon after we moved to the area, and it was there, on the quaint and rustic village ground, that I learned the game. Saturday afternoons meant cricket for the entire Fletcher family. Dad played, Barry and I went to watch, and Mum helped make the teas. I was still at junior school when I first had the chance of a game for the village. I always took my kit to the ground, and they were occasionally a man short, so I would bat at number eleven and field wherever my lack of inches was not too noticeable.

I used to go to the club during the week, too, and because I was so keen, the players took an interest and spent some time bowling at me. I particularly remember a man called Wally Carter, who was probably the best player in the village. He bowled off-breaks and could actually deliver them to order – quite an achievement at a level where most of the blokes thought the ball must have hit a bump if it deviated off line. Wally encouraged

8

me and I learned a lot from trying to cope with his bowling.

By the age of 11 I was a regular and serious member of the team, and subject to the same rules as everyone else. This meant I was expected to report for practice on Tuesdays and Fridays. The side for Saturday was never selected until the Friday evening and anybody who failed to appear on the ground that night was not considered. To be honest, practice took second place on Fridays to the preparation of the ground, which could be a lengthy business.

Caldecote CC's headquarters was, to all intents and purposes, a cowfield. The ground was covered in cowslips and buttercups and the square was simply cut out of the field and protected from the cows which grazed there all week by an electric fence, frequently out of service. First priority on Fridays, then, was to clear as much of the cowdung as possible to minimise the danger to fielders' flannels. Once that job was done, we could get down to the rolling and cutting of the pitch itself and only then squeeze in a bit of practice before the selectors met.

The setting was idyllic. The nearest road was half a mile distant, connected to the ground by a track. A stream ran down one side, and some imposing elm trees added to the kind of scene which typifies English village cricket at its best. Unfortunately, the wicket was also fairly typical, and I am glad, looking back, that our opponents rarely included any bowlers of devastating hostility!

In deference to my size I was put well down the order in my early games for Caldecote, but I did well enough to gain swift promotion and it was not too long before I was opening the batting, partnering my Dad. Between us, we discovered more than most about the standards of wickets in that part of the county, and I recall batting at the other end the day Dad was hit in the mouth by a ball which climbed unkindly off a spot the roller must have missed.

By the time I started playing for the village every week, Barry was also in the side. It is probably not unusual, in village cricket, for a father and his two sons to play simultaneously, but it seemed quite something to us. Barry had never taken to the game as I did, however. He didn't bowl and would usually bat at number eleven, playing his one shot with great regularity. It was an agricultural swing in the direction of mid-wicket and when he connected, which he managed to do about once in every six attempts, the ball would normally sail away into the elms. His great value to the side was as a fielder, in a department where we needed some improvement. Barry went on playing for Caldecote long after I moved on, but gave up the game after falling down a ladder and breaking his ankle.

Facilities at the Caldecote ground were virtually non-existent. There was a field, and a marked-out pitch. Nothing more. The creature comforts enjoyed by most of today's club cricketers, such as carpeted dressing-rooms, showers, lounge area and plush bars, could have been from another planet. There was not even anywhere to change at Caldecote – both teams had to turn up ready for action.

Our kit was hardly regulation dress, either. We never wore full whites, settling for something vaguely close, like grey trousers and a white dress shirt. Most of us considered ourselves privileged to have a pair of boots - tennis shoes were an accepted alternative. Other villages in the vicinity were just the same. It was our custom to turn up ready changed wherever we played, but on most occasions it was essential anyway.

After every match, home or away, we went to the village pub. We would still be in our cricket gear, because no one went home first, and we would generally be feeling a little sweaty as there was never anywhere to wash, let alone shower. But that could not spoil the evening, which was as much a part of cricket days as the match itself. I was always officially too young to drink while I played for Caldecote, but I never missed a night in the pub. I became very good at darts on those long summer evenings, because even if I had wanted to go home, I was stuck until the men decided to leave, normally at closing time.

Cricket was not part of the sporting curriculum at

school. In a school of so few masters and so few facilities, cricket was considered too difficult to organize satisfactorily. Anyway, there was really nowhere for us to play. We did play one game while I was there, and I was made captain, a job I also earned in the school football team. I played at inside-forward, to use an old-fashioned term, and in fact I continued to play soccer after leaving school. I turned out for village teams on Sunday mornings, but eventually grew tired of the syndrome. It always involved a bus journey into Cambridge and two lengthy searches – first to find your team's dressing-room in the endless corridors in the public park's pavilion, and then to discover which of the forty-odd pitches you had been allocated. Once I started to become known as an Essex cricketer, it seemed to be a challenge for some hulking defenders to work off their hangovers on me. On top of that, there were never any showers and I often used to go to the public baths to get cleaned up.

I gave up soccer at 18 and took up hockey instead, playing twice each weekend at good club standard for Royston and going on to play county hockey for Cambridgeshire at right-inner. This was a game I enjoyed far more, and I only stopped playing when I married and moved house at 24.

One thing I could not say about my school was that they discouraged me from cricket. On the contrary, although they could not provide me with any competitive element, they did provide me with a master who was to greatly influence my progress in the game. His name was Neville Rumbelow and, being a cricket addict and as disappointed as I was about the lack of school matches, he arranged some net sessions on an airstrip at an RAF camp near the school.

The surface was hard and very fast, and it taught me a great deal about contending with bounce and pace. It also instilled in Mr Rumbelow the idea that I had enough ability to make more of a life from cricket than I had shown I might make through any more academic channels, so thereafter he did his best to ensure that the school did not stand in my way.

11

He succeeded to the extent that I was given special privileges, the envy of any sports-mad schoolboy confined to his schoolroom. I had begun to play some mid-week matches for Royston, the nearest big club to my home. They played on Thursday afternoons and, although I was still only 13, the school agreed to let me off lessons each week so that I should not miss out on such good cricket. I have a suspicion that by then they had given up on my education, but it was still an appreciated gesture. Jeff Moss, one of the Royston players, travelled ten miles out of his way to pick me up at the school each Thursday lunchtime, so he is another person to whom I remain grateful.

Soon I began to play for Royston at weekends, chiefly in the second team initially. This meant the end of my playing association with Caldecote, and there were obviously regrets; but fortunately I am not the sentimental sort and, with the encouragement of my parents, I realized that I had to play senior club cricket if I were to make any appreciable progress at the game.

Neville Rumbelow was also responsible for my first contact with Essex. Unbeknown to me, he wrote to Trevor Bailey, who was both secretary and captain of the club at the time, suggesting my name for the County's Young Amateurs side. The nominations of schoolmasters are very important to counties, who, with limited finance, cannot be expected to have an infallible scouting system, and I was duly given a game against the Colchester and East Essex club during their cricket week. Once again, our coach took one look at the pint-sized specimen in front of him and decided I should bat low down the order, but any disappointment was muted because someone had decided I was a leg-spinner of some potential. I was given a long spell and took 5 wickets for 90-odd.

By the end of that season I had risen from number ten to six in the Young Amateurs batting, but I was still doing my share of bowling. Funnily enough, Mike Smith – later a prolific opening batsman for Middlesex – was in the opposition one day, and we were both considered far better prospects as spin bowlers than as batsmen.

Playing for the Young Amateurs would have been very difficult without the uncomplaining chauffering of my father. He was a sheet-metal worker, always out of the house by 8 a.m. and never home before 6 p.m. but he was quite willing and enthusiastic about taking time off to ferry me around.

His car was a 1938 Singer and for years its early-warning noises had been known among the lads of Caldecote. I was rarely at home in the evenings – there was always a made-up cricket match or a practice to attend somewhere in the village – and wherever my mates and I were playing, we could always hear Dad driving to the men's club, where he worked in the evenings. The brakes on the old Singer squealed appallingly, and had to be applied well before the target to ensure a safe halt.

That Singer broke down regularly, but fortunately my father's talents extended to a knowledge of motor mechanics, and no internal problems seemed to take him long to fix. If I had a match in London, or farther afield, he would spend the previous evening checking the car over, minimizing the risk of a panic.

After a summer of Young Amateurs games, I was invited to attend the Essex indoor school at Ilford for winter coaching. This was also a mid-week commitment and, once again, Bourne School was most obliging and I was excused lessons. It involved one day each week, and a long day too. I had to be up at 6.30 a.m. and on what the locals called the 'work bus' at 7 a.m. I then caught a train to London's Liverpool Street and a suburban train out east again to Gants Hill. From there it was just a walk around the corner to the cricket school, but the journey seldom took me much less than four hours. I was coached from 11 a.m. until about 2.30 p.m. and then I set off home again.

By now, my future was well mapped out – in my own mind anyway. I could not imagine wanting to do anything else but cricket, and I had decided that Essex must be the county for me. I was lucky that they came round to the same view.

I must have been a source of amusement to the well-healed seniors on the Essex staff when I was taken on – just 16, still tiny and very much from a rural background. Although I doubt if I admitted it to them, I had never even been on a county ground until I joined Essex. The only first-class cricket I had seen was at Cambridge University, and even those excursions had been rare as they involved a lengthy bus journey around most of the county's villages.

My only contact with the realities of the game at top level had come through avid reading of newspaper scores, and the occasional day spent watching Test matches at my friend's house – we had no television at ours. It was on that set in Caldecote that I saw Jim Laker's unforgettable 19 wickets against Australia in 1956. On that set I also admired from afar the great player whom I respected for almost three decades, until the day he phoned up to say he had sacked me as England captain – Peter May.

2

Petrol Pumps and Waterworks

In January of 1960, Fletcher's parents met Trevor Bailey, then the captain and secretary of Essex, to discuss their son's future. Bailey, impressed by what he had seen for himself and also by the judgements of respected coaches like Cyril Coote at Cambridge University, had decided that he wanted Fletcher on the Essex staff – despite the fact that he would not be 16 until May.

Keith needed no persuasion. He had left school, urged into his sporting life by the encouragement of Neville Rumbelow, and took up his duties on the Essex groundstaff on 25 April, suitably encouraged by the words of club coach Frank Rist. 'Keith is a natural cricketer,' said Rist, who had been with Essex almost thirty years. 'He is completely self-taught but I have no wish to change his style.'

Class distinction was rife when I joined Essex. To a wide-eyed 15-year-old realizing his first ambition in life, it did not seem wrong; I accepted it as a normal situation for the junior professionals to be segregated, silenced and generally dismissed by the seniors. I see it differently now.

A number of young lads joined the staff around the same time as myself. Among them were Robin Hobbs and Brian Edmeades, who were to be my team-mates for years to come when we all graduated to the county eleven. But in those early months together, we were all treated alike – as boys just out of school who were not really part of the club yet. The capped players had their own dressing-room and we were not allowed to enter unless

15

they wanted us for an errand. Our room was shared with the second-team capped staff, and there were times when it seemed we were scarcely allowed to speak to them.

Essex were not unusual. Most counties apparently operated that way in those days, and it occurs to me that a proportion of promising young cricketers must have dropped out of the game at an early stage, disillusioned by a system which cast them in such an undignified role.

Things have changed dramatically since then, of course, and I suspect we may even have gone slightly too far in the other direction, giving youngsters total freedom and equality when more discipline might not be a bad thing. But in general terms the change of attitude must be a good thing. If a player is good enough to be taken on the staff he should be encouraged to say what he thinks. He may be verbally shot down more often than not, but his personality will flourish far more readily that way than by being forced into the vows of silence we had to endure.

I am not suggesting that those in charge at Essex were all discriminatory ogres. Indeed, I quickly grew to like Trevor Bailey, who appeared to do every job at the club but remained an amateur player in the fashion of an earlier age. I also had a great respect for the senior professional, Ken Preston. He was from the old school, strict and firm, with set ideas on how the game should be played. But he was always fair to us youngsters and nobody could trample on us when he was around.

Most people think of Essex as a club which, for many years, existed on a shoestring squad of only thirteen or fourteen full-time professionals. But the financial problems which caused such severe cutbacks had still not materialized in the early sixties. When I joined, there were thirty on the staff. A lad like me, however promising, had to wait his turn, and it was two years before I made any significant progress. Or so I imagined. In fact, although I hardly played for the county sides at all until 1962, I was improving my game simply by learning from men like Trevor, Brian Taylor, Barry Knight and Jim Laker, with whom I could rub shoulders every day.

Until I went on the staff I had never been properly coached at all. The Caldecote players bowling at me on the cowfield, a few hints from Neville Rumbelow and the odd piece of advice from the experienced club cricketers of Royston made up the total of my tuition. Otherwise I had developed a style and technique by endless studying of a book called *The Art of Cricket* by Don Bradman. I tried to copy his shots from pictures, and stood for hours with a bat in front of a mirror, frequently cajoled and corrected by my father.

I never did quite emulate Bradman, but the personalized batting style served me well and, with hindsight, I am pleased that no one at Essex ever attempted to make radical changes. Too often, I have seen players who succeed without suiting conventional textbook ideals being forced to conform with orthodox styles, and suffering total loss of confidence as a result. I was left alone, apart from tips which concentrated more on tactics and attitude than technique.

There was a lot of local publicity about Essex taking me on, and one or two national papers even picked up the story of this little 15-year-old with big ideas. I think and hope I kept my feet firmly on the ground through it all. Certainly, no one ever accused me of being cocky, and those who are cocky normally have it pointed out to them.

I still played for Royston during 1960. Trevor Bailey advised me to play as much club cricket as possible and I took him literally, often playing as many as four games a week. The club on the heath at Royston has always been good to me and my contact with them has been maintained to this day. At the end of each season I go back and play a match or two for them, still enjoy it and still mix with many of the players who were in the side twenty years ago.

The harsher realities of life as a young county cricketer were brought home to me at the end of that year. Even if I had been filled with self-importance and dreaming of riches, a letter from Trevor Bailey was enough to restore my sense of perspective. In it he said the club was pleased with my progress, but added: 'Unfortunately, the county's

17

finances suffered a severe setback as a result of the weather and in consequence your winter retainer is very small. I shall be paying you a lump sum of £28 at the commencement of April.'

Clearly, I could not get by on that kind of money and, as I had reached the stage of no longer wanting to rely on my parents for support, I left home and went into digs. My first home was in the Ilford area, but I found I had no friends there so I moved to Leytonstone. It was hardly the smartest district of London, but its rough edges did me no harm. I had to stand on my own feet, and probably graduated to adulthood that winter, living as an individual for the first time and working in surroundings which were less than salubrious.

My job was menial but regular. I worked on the fore-court of a garage in the Lea Bridge Road, operating the petrol pumps. I cannot pretend I loved every minute of it, but the money was not bad and it certainly gave me the chance to meet plenty of people, if nothing else. Most days, I worked from 1 p.m. until 10 at night. When my shift finished, I caught the bus to Wanstead Cricket Club, which had become my regular night-time haunt. There was a good bar, with music, and I made a lot of friends there, although I never actually played for them.

The following April, I reported back to the sports ground at Fairlop where Essex always did their pre-season training. I use the word 'training' in a loose sense, because it was never applied as literally as it is around every county today. Essex in the early sixties were absurdly unprofessional by current standards. Any suggestion that the squad should train in the military style of physical exercise, now quite accepted, would have been greeted with disbelief and disdain. Gentle net sessions made up the professionals' programme until the county fixtures began and, inevitably, most of them were fat and unfit for the first few games.

Even on match days there was no question of limbering up before play. The team would turn up at the ground an hour before the start and fill in time by sitting around drinking tea. Fielding practice, which today occupies half an hour each morning for the Essex side, was never even contemplated.

This attitude persisted almost throughout the sixties and was probably only arrested by two things – Brian 'Tonker' Taylor becoming captain, and the John Player League starting up, with its inevitable demands on greater fitness. When Trevor was skipper, everything was taken at a leisurely pace. Superb cricketer though he was, Trevor probably suffered from never being able to accept that other players did not have his ability, and therefore needed to work harder to retain what talent they did have.

I saw the amateurish Essex outlook most clearly when the Gillette Cup began its illustrious life in 1963. This, surely, was an exciting new chance of honours, and the opportunity to win through to a final at a packed Lord's. But most of our staff did not see it that way. Instead, they regarded this new competition as an unwanted intrusion on their free days.

We were drawn against Lancashire at Old Trafford and did not even bother to book into a hotel. Instead, we were billeted out to various accommodating members of the Lancashire committee, just to save money. As a protest against the competition most of the team turned out in old kit; no one took the game seriously and we were soundly beaten, of course. What most dismayed me, as a keen young rookie, was the fact that the team seemed to rejoice in defeat because it ensured they would have several extra days off.

These enlightenments were still ahead of me, however, and in 1961 I was again content to play some club and ground games and continue with my club cricket. I was still living in Leytonstone and now split my weekends between two clubs. On Saturdays I played for South Essex Waterworks, who were a far stronger side than the unglamorous name might suggest. Eddie Presland, another newcomer to the Essex staff, also played for the club, and we were very difficult to beat.

One major change since those days is noticeable even in club cricket, and that is the unwillingness of anyone without a car to use public transport to a match – they just expect to be picked up and chauffered. My home matches for the Waterworks side, on their ground near Brentwood, involved a two-hour journey from Leytonstone, by tube and bus, and I was expected to make my own arrangements each week. If I couldn't get there, I wasn't picked. I was 18 by the time I took and passed my driving test and discovered how different life was with a car of my own. It was only an old Ford Popular, but it was reliable and I was independent. That meant a lot to a teenager in London.

By now I had grown a few inches and looked less like a deprived schoolboy. South Essex batted me regularly at number three and, significantly, hardly bowled me at all. My leg-breaks had been found out!

My Sunday cricket was played for a club called Lennox, based in Leytonstone and containing a high proportion of professional footballers. Tottenham's Eddie Baily and Ted Ditchburn and quite a number of West Ham players, including Alan Sealey and Ronnie Boyce, turned out most weeks for Lennox, and as the opposition was always strong the cricket was of a high and enjoyable standard.

I didn't go home once that summer. Never seemed to have the time. It was an idyllic existence to me, spending weekdays playing and practising with Essex and the weekends on the club grounds of the county. I wondered if it might suddenly all end and I would have to get a real job!

Essex had no playing base at that time. The club's offices were at Chelmsford, where our rapidly expanding ground stands now, but we played no more matches there than at our numerous other 'homes' around the county. Leyton, Ilford, Romford, Brentwood, Clacton, Colchester and Westcliff all hosted games and I am not sure that the nomadic element was good for the side, however convenient it may have been for our far-flung supporters. County teams do play better in familiar conditions, but we were such gypsies in the sixties that no conditions ever became familiar to us. We still play festival weeks at Ilford, Colchester and Southend today, but the great majority of our games are at Chelmsford and this, I feel, has been a contributory factor, if only slight, in the recent successes of the team.

I played my first games for the county in 1962. They registered me to play in Championship cricket and discovered a problem they had not anticipated – my birthplace. The Essex officials had assumed I was born in Cambridgeshire, a Minor County and therefore an open hunting-ground for any first-class club. When it was established that I originated from Worcester, Essex had to go through the formalities of seeking permission from their counterparts at Worcestershire, who had an automatic first claim on my services. Fortunately for my peace of mind, if not for my ego, Worcester raised no objections and I was duly registered. At the time, however, I was quite prepared for the possibility of an entire season in the second team.

That was certainly how it began, but a little rash of half-centuries, allied to the confidence always shown in me by Trevor Bailey, meant that I was the logical deputy batsman when Barry Knight was recruited to Test cricket for England. The call came in the last week of July. A three-day game against Glamorgan, in Ebbw Vale of all places. Essex had just finished a match at Colchester on the Tuesday evening, and I set off on the long journey across country to Wales, with Trevor in the driving seat. It was hardly the ideal preparation for my county début, as we arrived at the hotel at 3.30 on Wednesday morning. A few hours of sleep and we were on the field, having lost the toss.

I am not the type who has a photographic memory for the scores in every past match, but this one remains clear in my mind. Glamorgan, with the basis of the side which won the County Championship seven years later, were skittled out for 64 by Trevor and Ken Preston, so by mid-afternoon on the first day I was at the crease for my first Championship innings.

Trevor had put me at number seven, a sensible position for a young newcomer, especially in such tricky conditions, and we were 60-odd for 5 when I made my entrance.

21

I scored 11 before falling to that fine seam bowler, later to become a Test selector, Ossie Wheatley.

We led by only 41 on the first innings and then produced an abysmal bowling performance. Jim Presdee, always an under-rated cricketer, played marvellously for 100 and the Welshmen reached 252. It always looked too many for us, and we were beaten by 81 runs. Not a dream début, then, although I made 27 in the second innings, enough to keep my place for the game at Sheffield which began the following day.

3

French Follies

Living in London was all very well, but for the rurally-reared Fletcher it meant a temporary end to the pleasurable pastimes of his childhood and teens, country pursuits such as hunting, shooting and even ferreting. It also meant he was conducting a long-distance romance . . . but his Essex career began to flourish nevertheless. In 1964 he made his maiden first-class century, against Lancashire at Old Trafford, and soon the first noises were heard of what was to become a clamorous campaign to win him international honours. That, though, was still a distant dream.

If I did not read the cricket press, my mother would, so I always knew whenever my name was praised. It did surprise me, though, that certain people were pushing me for England selection as early as 1964, by which time I had played only two full seasons for Essex. Nowadays, for various reasons, that would hardly raise an eyebrow, but England's batting order was far more established in the early sixties. I was still a rookie, and quite prepared to wait for my turn.

I comfortably topped 1000 runs in each of those first two seasons, and the other landmarks arrived steadily. My first century was made against an attack which included Brian Statham and Sonny Ramadhin, and, by chance, two other players who were to feature prominently in my later career made their own maiden centuries on the same day – my Essex team-mate Brian Edmeades, and Warwickshire's Dennis Amiss, with whom I was to play much of my Test cricket.

That season holds further good memories. I was chosen

for the President of MCC's XI against the Australian tourists, which was my first senior representative honour and the first clue that I might be in the minds of England selectors. Then, to the surprise of most, Essex defeated the Australians at Southend – thrashed them in fact. It might not have been the strongest Australian side to ever play here, but they won the Ashes series 1–0 so it ranked as a great achievement for the county. A good match for me, too, as I scored a century in the first innings and was then at the crease when we completed the 6-wicket win.

Essex's financial position remained precarious, however. We were down to a shoestring staff of a dozen by the mid-sixties and continued to struggle in the middle reaches of the Championship. At the time, although I wanted success, it did not seem as lamentable a state of affairs as it does now, with the benefit of almost twenty years' hindsight.

I was living at home again by this stage. At least, I spent the small amount of free time available there. There was little chance to relax by going shooting or fishing, or pursuing any of the other hobbies which I had grown into as a boy.

Being brought up in farming country, I did many things that would completely puzzle town boys. Ferreting, for instance. The theory, of course, is to put a ferret down a rabbit hole, which brings an anguished rabbit racing out of his warren and into a net which has been placed over the hole. We had to learn the technical details, such as the need to do it away from roots and trees and preferably on sandy banks which, fortunately, were abundant in our part of Cambridgeshire. We also had to learn how to hit the rabbit on the head, killing it instantly. They then needed to be immediately gutted before we sold them in the district. We bred the ferrets ourselves and, as lads will, often ventured on to private property in search of rabbit holes. Many were the times that we had to show a good turn of foot as an angry farmer gave chase. If the sport seems cruel to anyone, though, I can only say that killing rabbits was never seen as doing anything but good in our area, and that ferreting was simply the old, country manner of spending a Sunday morning.

My early life, in fact, when I look back, seems dominated by animals. I kept thirty rabbits and a number of guinea pigs in the garden of our house. Less conventionally, I also kept goats and, as a young schoolboy, got out of bed at 6.30 each morning to milk them. I tried to develop my own milk round, selling the goats' milk in jugs after I had boiled it, but if I am honest, most of it was bought by my mother!

Our eight-acre grounds, only just accessible by car up a narrow, bumpy pathway, also housed some pheasants which I undertook to feed. This had to be carried out at the same time each day, to get them used to the routine. Pigeon-shooting was often on my agenda, and occasionally I would help out with the gamekeeping, trapping stoats.

As a complete contrast, I went regularly to ballroom dancing classes. I am not quite sure why, and I am certain I did not enjoy it much, but if it did only one thing for my future life it was to introduce me to Sue, who is now my wife.

Each week I went to dancing class with one of my best pals. His name was Peter Agshead and he was rough and scruffy. We fought like hell, but always ended up friendly again, although his rebellious tendencies stretched to turning up for ballroom dancing in muddy wellington boots. The attraction for me of dancing, however, was the presence of a girl called Pat who lived in Caldecote. I was 16, she was about the same age, and we had begun going out together. Most weekends she got together with her great friend Sue, who lived four miles away in Great Eversdon and normally rode over to Caldecote on her bike. Occasionally, I would be invited too, and it soon struck me that I was getting on just as well with Sue as with Pat – in fact, rather better. Some years later, after the usual traumas of teenage romances had been overcome, we got married – I was even prepared to forgive the fact that she was a Yorkshire girl!

By that time, Essex cricket had undergone a transformation and my own career was just taking off at international level. Neither event was unconnected with Brian Taylor who, while doing so much to invigorate Essex, also provided me with a great deal of encouragement and advice at a crucial stage of my development. 'Tonker', as he was always known to us, seems to have been landed with a reputation for being a hard man with a loud voice. The second part is certainly true, but I would dispute the first. He is a kind, rather sensitive man who would give his last pound to any of his friends who were in trouble.

He took over the captaincy of the side in 1967 when Trevor Bailey retired. Although we had the makings of a useful team, the economy cuts had now reached such a drastic stage that it was not a job anyone could envy. I remember our secretary of the time, a retired major named Charles Brown, being quoted as saying: 'Wherever I could save five shillings a night on the team's hotel expenses, I have done so.' By that, it is easy to appreciate that we were not exactly wrapped in cotton-wool luxury. Add to that the facts that the club and ground team in which I had played only a few years earlier had been scrapped, the second-team commitments pruned, and groundstaff and ancillary part-timers reduced in numbers, and the club's plight becomes plainer.

But we were happy to experiment. We were the first county to try Sunday play in Championship games and the venture worked so well that it acted as an encouragement for the subsequent formation of the John Player League, the competition which finally buried our reputation as a no-hope outfit.

In the meantime, however, we had made steady improvements in the Championship. A few of today's team had appeared, including David Acfield, John Lever and Stuart Turner, who had been sacked by Trevor after the 1965 season but was brought back eighteen months later to the benefit of everyone who has played for us since. We still did not have enough good players – that would have been difficult with a total of only twelve on the staff – but through the natural adversities of a small squad, and the growling defiance of our new captain, the famed Essex team spirit was born.

One of the inevitable consequences of having such a tight squad is that on many occasions injuries had to be ignored. The slight pains, twists and pulls which in these enlightened, more fortunate days of large staffs would necessitate a week's lay-off, simply meant a bit of discomfort on the field. We played on with the injuries because, if we had not, Essex would either have taken the field short, or had to call in local club players. 'Tonker' was the only wicketkeeper on the staff, for instance, and I clearly recall him playing more than once with chipped fingers and other minor ailments. Only once in my time did he miss a match – and that was through a pulled hamstring which would have put most players out for a fortnight.

We did not have a great season that first year under Taylor. Trevor played less than half the matches before, at 43 years old, accepting total retirement, and with Barry Knight having left an enormous hole in our talent by resigning to join Leicestershire, struggle was inevitable. We won only three matches and the bright spots came chiefly from the newcomers – names which were to become synonymous with Essex cricket in years to come: David Acfield, Robin Hobbs, Ray East and Keith Boyce.

Only two teams, Glamorgan and Gloucestershire, those perennial strugglers, finished below us in the County Championship, but we ended a disappointing season with a remarkable flourish. We went to the big bowl of a ground at Scarborough in festival week, the first week in September, with the holidaymakers packing themselves in to watch their beloved Yorkshire collect the points they needed for yet another county title. But it did not work out that way. Yorkshire needed only 119 to beat us, but in one of the tensest Championship finishes I can recall, they fell 9 short – bowled out by the off-spin of Acfield and the leg-breaks of Hobbs. 'Accers', who was only just 20 and still at Cambridge, took 5 wickets in a marathon spell to bring us a victory which seemed sweet enough at the time. Looking back, after all I have been through since at the hands of the Yorkshire public, it seems like perfection. Even the fact that Yorkshire recovered their composure enough to win the Championship for the sixth time in nine years did not matter. We had enjoyed our day of glory.

By now, I would have needed to be blind not to notice that I was on the very verge of a Test cap. I had been to Pakistan the previous winter with an MCC Under-25 side under Mike Brearley and now, in 1967, I had easily improved on my previous efforts for Essex and made more than 1600 runs. The tour that winter was to the West Indies, and of course I crossed my fingers and hoped. But the selectors decided I was not quite ready, and that was a decision I respected. In my heart I might have even agreed. Another winter of waiting did me no harm, anyway.

I began it by being picked to play inside-right for the Cambridgeshire hockey side. For some years I had played regular hockey for Royston, and enjoyed it to a degree where I would like to have taken it more seriously, but saw even then the dangers of trying to split my attention between two sports.

Even playing for Royston meant maintaining a good club standard; promotion into county hockey involved far greater demands on fitness and concentration, enjoyable though it was. I continued with the game until I was 24 and then, on marrying Sue, gave it up, but that winter of 1967-8 I played only half a season, having accepted an invitation to spend three months in the East with an international cricket side, managed by Joe Lister and captained by Mickey Stewart.

The tour began in Sierre Leone and ended in Hong Kong, stopping off in India, Pakistan, Sri Lanka and a number of other exotic hotspots. It involved a good deal of travelling but I found it a marvellous experience. The Englishmen in the side were all on the fringe of the Test side – Dennis Amiss, Jack Birkenshaw, Mike Denness and Tony Greig spring to mind – and I was immensely impressed by the leadership of Mickey Stewart. A great organizer and a great professional. Knowing him as I do

now, it is no surprise that Surrey have rediscovered the
habit of winning with Mickey back at the Oval as
manager.

I returned for the home season of 1968 feeling good. I
had made a century in Karachi against a strong Pakistan
Board XI and thought I had probably done enough runs
for Essex, pushing myself into the public gaze. If it is true
that certain counties are more fashionable than others,
and therefore more likely to attract the interest of Test
selectors, then Essex was certainly not. Since the depar-
tures of Bailey and Knight we had been left with a side
without a Test cap between them and we were still considered a rather downbeat outfit. Let's face it, we had
nine home grounds and it was necessary for anyone, even
a selector, to do some homework if he were to turn up on
the right ground to find us.

'Tonker' was as indomitable as ever. One thing that is
true about him is the amount of noise he made. His
philosophy appeared to be 'the louder I shout, the more
they will jump for me', and he put it into practice with
great gusto on and off the field. To newcomers I am sure
it was disconcerting, but all those of us who had been at
the club a few years were well aware that this was a
genuine case of bark being far worse than bite.

On the field he was anything but the autocrat he has
sometimes been made out to be. His great quality was a
willingness to listen to the views of others; I have yet to
meet a good captain who tried to do everything alone.
'Tonker' knew that his tactical sense was not brilliant,
and he consulted all his senior players. By his later years
in charge, I was doing much of the field placement myself,
and he was happy for this to develop. But never did he
hide behind someone else if the stick were flying. If we
had been beaten when victory seemed easier, he took the
kicks himself.

I have to say that he was not the off-field disciplinarian
many people seem to imagine, either. We were a young,
lively team and, to be honest, we were often allowed to
get away with murder. Now and again 'Tonker' would
make the token effort of imposing a curfew and even

29

staying up himself to ensure that it was respected. It was on one of these purges that Ray East was caught out, and despite the catalogue of stories surrounding 'Easty' ever since, this one still stands out in my mind as being the funniest.

We were playing Hampshire at Bournemouth during the 1968 season if I remember correctly. Roy Marshall and Barry Richards had both made big scores against us, and we had then been bowled out cheaply. 'Tonker' stuck out his chin and insisted that everyone was in bed by 11 p.m. as we were not going to be beaten.

Our base was called the South Western, an old-fashioned railway hotel next to the main Bournemouth station. It had spartan rooms but an outstanding restaurant so most of us, deciding to abide by our leader's orders, ate in the hotel and went to bed meekly. 'Tonker', however, had noticed that not everyone was present and he intended to get to the bottom of it. He prowled around the foyer for some while and then took a stroll outside, whereupon he discovered the bizarre sight of someone climbing up the drainpipe. It had to be Raymond East, just 21 years old but already a joker and an eccentric. By a fine piece of mountaineering he was already above the first floor heading for his room on the second when 'Tonker's' stentorian voice froze him. How he did not let go and fall down, I shall never know. All I will stress is that this particular Ray East tale is absolutely true.

One other memorable incident of that vintage occurred during a match against Kent at Dover. David Bradford, a director of Townsend-Thoresen ferries and a keen Essex supporter, suggested it would be a fun idea for the team to go across to France the following night, have a meal and return to Dover. We would all be back in decent time, he assured us.

Most teams, of course, would not even have entertained the idea in the middle of a Championship match. But we did. Almost the entire side took him up on the suggestion and enjoyed rather more than a quiet meal. By the time we had sampled some of the night-time delights of northern France and tottered back on to the boat, it was approaching three in the morning and one or two among our number were decidedly the worse for wear. 'Tonker' could hardly object to our indiscipline this time, however, as he was with us!

Our results continued to conform to an eccentric pattern, although the first half of that season saw us achieve a more respectable position in the table than we had been growing accustomed to. Keith Boyce was making a visible difference to our attack, and although John Lever was still very young, his promise was evident already.

The batting, however, was weak – certainly when compared to our modern side and the likes of Graham Gooch, Kenny McEwan and company. At 24 years old I found I was carrying a hefty burden of run-making, and if I failed, we were too often pitched out for poor scores. Fortunately, I had run into my richest form yet, averaging almost 50 over the first third of the season. That first Test cap was now a priority, and with the Australians in England, what better way to start?

One particular innings, I recall, probably persuaded the selectors that I was worth a chance. It came on a dreadful pitch at Southchurch Park in Southend which the umpires – Bert Alderman and Laurie Gray – reported to MCC as being unfit for first-class cricket. Our opponents were Middlesex, and 40 wickets fell in two days for 446 runs as the ball bounced unevenly and turned in an exaggerated manner.

When I went out to bat, for the second time in the match, Essex were 9 for 2, just 33 runs ahead. John Price was breathing fire and we soon became 11 for 3 and then, as the spinners joined in the fun, 40 for 8. At that point we seemed to be in a hopeless position, but I was joined by Ray East and somehow we put on 74 for the ninth wicket. Last man John Lever stuck around, too, and another 19 were added before I was out to Peter Parfitt for 84. Not the biggest, but certainly one of the most taxing and satisfying innings I had played that season, and it grew in significance as East and Boyce bowled out Middlesex for 69, to bring victory by 88 runs.

The Test series got under way without me. England,

captained by Colin Cowdrey, were well beaten at Old Trafford, but might have won at Lord's had it not been for the interference of the weather. But Australia had come to England in possession of the Ashes, so had only to draw the series in order to retain them. We needed to win at least two of the three remaining Tests to deprive them, and changes were widely anticipated for the third match at Edgbaston. I waited, often seeing my name bandied around the press but not daring to take anything for granted.

When it came, the call was couched in the refined, rather pompous tones one comes to associate with MCC: a stereotyped letter, the customary means of confirming selection to all England players in those days, with space left blank for one's name.

It read: 'Dear Keith, The Board of Control Selection Committee will be glad if you will report to the England captain on the ground at Edgbaston not later than 3pm on Wednesday 10th July and be available to play for England v Australia, if selected, on 11th–16th July, 1968. The players and selectors will dine together on the evening of 10th July 1968.'

After a stern paragraph forbidding players to comment to the press on the match, arrangements concerning the hotel, travel and finance were outlined. We were to stay at The Raven Hotel, in Droitwich, the traditional base for Birmingham Tests at the time, and in addition to our travelling and accommodation being paid, the MCC undertook to allow each player the sum of £3 for incidental expenses and £1 for each meal taken outside the hotel. Can that really be only fifteen years ago?

The scale of fees ranged from £120 for those who played to £65 for the twelfth man and £25 for reserves. What is interesting is that this did not dramatically improve until almost ten years later, when Cornhill's sponsorship gave Test players an overnight pay rise of 500 per cent.

The letter, which filled both sides of a foolscap sheet, went on to explain medical arrangements, allotment of complimentary tickets and the need to send an immediate telegram to confirm fitness and availability. But the impersonal nature of it all was balanced by a handwritten note to me from Doug Insole, once an Essex player and then the chairman of selectors. It just said 'Well played. Good luck', but it was a nice touch, typical of the man.

Looking at the makeup of the England twelve, I guessed there was a good chance I would be twelfth man, and I was right. But I did not have long to wait.

4

The Horror of Headingley

England drew the third Test at Edgbaston, with Fletcher acting as drinks waiter. Now if the Ashes were to be regained, the last two Tests had to be won, and the omens were not hopeful as both Geoff Boycott and Colin Cowdrey reported injuries. Boycott was ruled out, but Cowdrey, the captain, was included in the squad of thirteen named for the Headingley Test. Roger Prideaux was to win his first cap as Boycott's deputy, there was a romantic recall for Ted Dexter, and a place in the party for Fletcher. This time, he was to see action, but the story had an unpleasant twist.

For as long as I live I shall never forget my Test début, but I am afraid I remember it for all the wrong reasons. Even now, when I think back, I feel traces of bitter resentment that what should have been one of the greatest weeks of my life was soured beyond belief.

My anger is not directed at any other player, nor even caused directly by anything which occurred on the field. It is the result of the diabolical treatment I was given by the people who are supposed to be the most appreciative and knowledgeable cricket watchers in the land. The Yorkshire public left me sickened and disillusioned, and I have never forgiven them.

Before detailing the match, and all its peripheral unpleasantness for this particular young débutant, it is essential to describe the background to the team selection. Cowdrey, who had a torn thigh muscle, was never likely to play, the fitness test arranged for the eve of the match being no more than a gesture aimed partly at leaving the opposition guessing. Ted Dexter, who had decided to

make himself available for Sussex again and guaranteed
a Test return with a double-century against Kent, was to
bat at three and the last place, at number six, was between
Barry Knight, my old Essex colleague and myself. I
understood I was likely to play, with Dexter being used
as third seamer.

Complications arose, however, when Tom Graveney,
Cowdrey's deputy as captain, reported on the Wednesday
morning that he had split a thumb. His availability was
open only to slight doubt, but the selectors decided that
a standby was necessary and Philip Sharpe was sum-
moned from Westcliff, where he was already batting for
Yorkshire against Essex. It was the natural choice, Sharpe
being an experienced, solid batsman, but it was to lead,
indirectly, to much of my suffering.

For reasons known only to themselves, most Yorkshiremen appeared to assume that, once in the squad, Sharpe
would play. When he did not, Graveney recovering suf-
ficiently as expected, they seemed preoccupied with finding a subject on which to vent their wrath. They found
me.

Things went badly for us from the outset. Graveney
lost the toss to Barry Jarman, another substitute skipper
in the absence of Bill Lawry, and we were inevitably
consigned to the field. I quickly received my first surprise
when Tom, setting the field for John Snow, directed me
to first slip. This, of course, was where Cowdrey would
normally field, and we clearly had a problem there, but
I could not help thinking it was taking a chance to put
me there, in my first Test, when my only previous experience of the position had been the odd occasion when
spinners were bowling for Essex.

Almost all my close fielding had been confined to third
slip and short-leg, positions where one has to watch the
batsman and concentrate on his backlift and foot movement. First slip is entirely different. There, it is essential
to look at the bowler as well as the batsman, and for
someone unused to it, the transition can be very difficult.

It was at this point, virtually before the game had
begun, that the crowd started on me. Their hero Sharpe

happened to be just about the best first slip in England at the time, and they interpreted my presence there as being an insult to him. Obtuse thinking, maybe, but that did not worry them. The chants for Sharpe began, and were to reach their mocking crescendo before too long.

'Snowy' bowled beautifully with the new ball. He gave us a great start by bowling John Inverarity cheaply and passed the outside edge time and again. Then, on two occasions, he found the edge and both times the ball flew within my catching range. The first was to my left and needed a forward dive, the second was sharp, low and to my right. I got my hands to them both, but they went down.

You can imagine how I felt. First Test, first day, and the first thing I had done for England was to drop two catches. No matter how hard they might have been, I still felt low. At times like that any cricketer needs some understanding and encouragement from his team-mates, and some sympathy from the crowd, because no one willingly drops a catch. Instead, although nobody on the field was less than diplomatic, the Yorkshire crowd changed the tempo of their barracking and became shamefully abusive.

Ian Redpath and Ian Chappell both made big scores and it was lunchtime on the second day by the time Australia were dismissed for 315. I was down to bat at six, and it seemed I would have a long wait as John Edrich and Prideaux put on 123 for the first wicket, Prideaux starting his Test career rather more happily than I was doing by scoring 64. Three wickets then fell for 18 runs, including Dexter for a disappointing 10, and I was padded up, ready to go in for what promised to be an unpleasant last hour of the day. Fortunately, or so I thought, Graveney and Kenny Barrington saw it through to the close and I had another night to think about my innings.

That fourth-wicket stand took the score to 209, so we were in a healthy position when the waiting ended and I walked out to the middle. The crowd's reception was anything but warm, but I tried to ignore it. I survived an over or two and then, facing Alan Connolly, got into position to leg-glance as his line strayed. The ball brushed my thighpad – nothing else, I swear to this day – and Jarman went up with all the slips as he took it down the legside. Syd Buller's finger was already raised as I looked up, and it did not take long for the crowd to celebrate. Yes, celebrate the dismissal of an England batsman. I could hardly believe it.

All the unhappy way back to the pavilion, I was subjected to booing and jeering which made me sad and angry in about equal measures. Some idiot even ran on to the field to taunt me from close quarters. One Englishman abusing another in an Ashes series: it was beyond my comprehension.

The feeling that an injustice had been done did not improve my mood, and when I read the Sunday papers the next morning, probably fearing a panning from the critics, I was interested in Godfrey Evans's comment article in the *People*. Questioning Buller's decision, he wrote: 'Jarman hardly had to move to take the ball. I could not see, from my 91-Test experience of wicketkeeping, how Jarman could have taken the ball so easily if Fletcher had got a nick trying to play it away on the legside.' Cold comfort, but it was still nice to know I was not the only one debating the decision. Sadly, it was in the book, and I had joined the reluctant band of cricketers who have begun their Test careers with a duck. The first emotion I experienced was the natural, if irrational, panic that I may never get another chance.

As it turned out, my second opportunity arrived on the final afternoon of the Headingley Test but it gave me little more pleasure than the first. We had been set 326 to win in just short of five hours, and if we had achieved that it would have featured among the greatest Test wins of modern times. But, after Prideaux had gone early, we were carried into contention by Erich and Dexter. Graveney then made a swift 41 but the odds were always against us, and the chase was called off when our fourth wicket fell at 168. Graveney, the man out, passed me as I walked to the middle and his instructions were confusing, to say the least: 'Play for a draw,' he said, 'but make it look good.'

I concentrated on the first part of the order and, in company with Barrington, saw us through to the close at 230 for 4. With 23 not out, I reasoned that I had done my job. It was dull, I knew, but the alternative was a pointless sacrifice of wickets. But the crowd once again saw things differently and completed my nightmare match by pouring on to the ground at the end with the sole object of jeering at me. Barrington, who had been in far longer and had not played appreciably differently, was ignored; I was the man they wanted to insult, and they made a comprehensive job of it.

There is no point in pretending it did not affect or upset me. Back in the dressing-room, I was terribly low. I had been through six days of hell thanks to that crowd; the dropped catches and the duck I could have coped with, but the vindictive barracking was different.

Some of the other England players tried to console me and point out that I had done all that was asked of me. But, in truth, there was no great spirit in the Test side at that time. Most of the players had an individualistic outlook and tended to look after themselves, which meant there was little of the camaraderie which marks the England teams of recent years.

I went off to my next county match feeling angrier all the time. I have not yet forgiven or forgotten that experience, and it seems that the Yorkshire public have long memories, too, for even now they are hostile towards me. A few years ago I scored a good hundred on a wet pitch at Middlesbrough. If the spectators there had been as knowledgeable as we southerners are always led to believe, they would have appreciated the value of the innings and at the very least had the decency to keep quiet. But no, the jeering went on as ever before, and at the end I needed a police escort out of the ground through crowds of drunken louts who wanted to pick an argument if not a fight.

Even at Scarborough, where the audience is largely drawn from a different group from those who patronize

Headingley, the bug has been caught and I am the favourite target. To my mind, Yorkshire crowds have behaved disgracefully towards me and it is tempting to generalize and express a contempt for everyone born in the county. But I must say their players, with only the odd exception, have generally been extremely friendly and highly embarrassed by the saga. Time after time, they have apologized to me when the usual outburst of booing greets my arrival, and wicketkeeper David Bairstow once said: 'I see you've brought all your mates with you again.'

It has a quite different effect on me these days, however. I no longer feel hurt or angry. The barrackers are not worth the bother. But the way they behave has filled me with the motivation to succeed at Yorkshire's expense. I take immense satisfaction from beating Yorkshire on their own patch and I have even reached the stage where I enjoy playing there and revel in the aggressive atmosphere. One of my best recent memories, however, is of a home game against them, in the semi-final of the Benson and Hedges Cup. Thousands of Yorkshiremen had made the long journey down to Chelmsford and it gave me great pleasure to think we had sent them home with only a defeat to talk about.

One of the ironies of the events of 1968 is that I was dropped after the Headingley match, and the next time I figured in an England squad for a home Test was for the third and final match against the West Indies the following summer – at, of all places, Leeds.

I could not complain about being left out, even if to give any batsman a one-match baptism seems mean and is nowadays chiefly avoided. At least, however, I was able to repair my shaken confidence back in the more sedate environment of county cricket, and this I did to some effect with a double-century against Sussex at Hastings, which to date is still the highest score of my career. I made 228 not out against an attack lacking John Snow, and Essex were able to register the rare triumph of an innings win.

Those runs could hardly have come at a more opportune time for me, as the Test series was over and the selectors had turned their attention to picking a party for the scheduled winter tour of South Africa.

It was announced in the last week of August, earlier than is now the custom, and my name was on the list. But it was a name that was missing which was to lead cricket into a major political row, culminating in the cancellation of the tour, and longer-term, in the breaking off of all our cricketing relations with South Africa. Basil D'Oliveira was not included, despite scoring a century in the final Test of the Australian series, and when, some weeks later, he was named as the replacement in the party following an injury to Tom Cartwright the South African government refused to allow him entry. The upshot of it all is part of cricket history. In practical terms, it meant that the England party, D'Oliveira included, had Christmas at home and then set off on a trip to Pakistan which, to most of us, was not quite so appealing as South Africa.

In the meantime, the home season had wound up in the traditional manner with the Scarborough Festival, then still at the peak of its appeal and attracting the cream of available players and daily crowds of around 10,000. I accepted invitations to play in all three matches – for England against the Rest of the World, for England Under-25s against an England XI, and for MCC against Yorkshire.

Going back to Yorkshire for the first time since the Headingley Test, my mind was naturally full of conflicting thoughts. The one clear thing in my head was that I badly wanted to show these Yorkshiremen that I could play. By making centuries for the Under-25s and MCC, I achieved that in the best possible way, and left Yorkshire in a far happier frame of mind than I had done a month earlier.

5

Pakistan, 1969 – the Worst Tour Ever?

Some cricketers take eagerly and happily to the unusual life de-
manded of a regular winter tourist. For others, the months spent
away from home are disagreeable, sometimes barely tolerable. But
Keith Fletcher has maintained an equable and enthusiastic attitude
to touring, and has enjoyed every country to which cricket has taken
him – with one notable exception: Pakistan. His dislike of that
country was generated by the England tour of 1969, a reluctant
substitution for the planned trip to South Africa. It began with
crowd riots in Lahore and ended prematurely when the England
squad sensibly decided they had taken more than enough
disturbances.

As I see things now I would never again undertake a tour
of Pakistan. I say that on the unforgettable evidence of
trips which gave me the most frightening experiences of
my life. It is most unlikely that I will be asked to go
again, but if the occasion arose, I would decline. A Test
tour to Pakistan is planned for the winter of 1983–4, and
I only hope there will be fewer troubles than previously.

The same problems have cropped up every time I have
been to Pakistan. Much of the cricket has been boring;
some of the facilities have been poor. The public, unlike
their friendly and fanatical Indian neighbours, are sometimes hostile to Englishmen and seem almost not to be
interested in cricket. Perhaps worst of all, Test matches
have been ruined by crowd trouble in almost every Test
centre.

I doubt whether any cricket tour has ever been as unpleasant as our 1969 visit to Pakistan. I know the lads who went to the West Indies in 1981 had a very rough time, with disasters punctuating the trip both on and off the field. But the 1969 tour lasted only six weeks, and each of them seemed like a month.

It was my first England tour and nothing could have been better designed to put me off the life of a Test player. Politicians caused the cancellation of the South African trip to which everyone was looking forward; now politics wrecked the hurriedly-arranged stand-in affair, to which nobody was looking forward, although one realized that it was done mainly to provide us with winter employment.

I feel that the tour should never have taken place. Despite the short notice, I suggest that with a little more foresight and the advice of the right people, it would have been obvious before we ever left London. Pakistan was engaged in virtual civil war, and the east of the country was under student law. Somehow, we were expected to go out there and perform as if the setting were Lord's in June and the distractions no more threatening than a few Taverners with too many pints inside them. It was tantamount to being asked to bat with a gun at our heads; sometimes, indeed, that was almost literally the case.

Every one of the three Tests was interrupted by riots. Everywhere we went, we were protected by armed guards – except for one bizarre day in Karachi when the students insisted that they were removed and the frightened authorities hastily agreed. There were occasions, I admit, when I thought we had little chance of getting home safely, and some players were affected far more severely than I.

The trip began quietly enough, with a ten-day sojourn in Ceylon, as it was then called. This, of course, was long before the country was even seriously considered for full Test status, and the programme of one three-day game and three one-day matches was designed primarily to play us into form, bearing in mind that most of the fifteen tourists had not played competitively for four months or more.

Even on this gentle introduction to the trip, however, things went wrong, the most serious being an elbow injury to Jeff Jones which ended his tour and his England career. This was a tragedy, for Jeff was not only one of the best left-arm pace bowlers I have ever seen, but also a smashing bloke. For us, it was just the start of our problems. Things were to get very much worse before too long.

Even before we landed in Pakistan, we had a taste of the chaos to come. The situation was so bad in the east of the country that the first part of the tour needed wholesale reshaping. We were to have played a first-class match in Chittagong before taking an internal flight on to Dacca, venue for the first Test. But while we were still in Colombo, our manager Les Ames had the first of many meetings with High Commissioners, and emerged poker-faced with the news that both these places were so torn by rioting that the games would inevitably be moved. You can imagine just what effect this had on our players, some of whom had been openly apprehensive of the situation in Pakistan before we had even set off from home. The strength of manager Ames was crucial, even at this early stage, because Colin Cowdrey as captain was already showing what I thought were signs of weakness amid the hostility.

The first Test was switched to Lahore, which at least meant we would be accommodated in the top-class Intercontinental Hotel. It provided few other comforts, as we were very soon to discover. The student-rule situation was by no means confined to one sector of the country, and their authority extended to the ridiculous extent that Pakistan were forced to include a student leader, 21-year-old Aftab Gul, in their side. To be fair to him, Aftab was not a bad player and he showed some inclination to keep his colleagues in the crowd under an element of control. But the principle was absurd — can you imagine university students taking over English cricket and insisting that an Oxford freshman played in every Test of a major series?

If I had been labouring under any delusions that all would be well once the serious cricket began, these were dispelled by the opening day of the series. England closed at 226 for 5 but in the course of the day I had twice been set upon by members of the crowd as I walked to the wicket and, just to add insult to injury, I had also been given out, caught off my boot.

There were only 10,000 in the ground, whereas on the Under-25s tour under Mike Brearley a couple of years earlier we had regularly played before crowds of 50,000. Yet those who were at Lahore seemed far more intent on disrupting the cricket than enjoying it.

Cowdrey made a century, admirably determined in the circumstances, and I shared a stand of 69 with him. But I admit my mind was not as riveted on the cricketing job as it should have been. When I walked out to start my innings I was accompanied by a number of student fans, hardly a circumstance to settle a young man in only his second Test, and when Cowdrey and I went out to resume after tea we were jostled by dozens of spectators and I was almost dragged to the ground. It was an absolute shambles and the police seemed powerless to do anything about it.

Two descriptions by Michael Melford in the *Daily Telegraph* sum up my feelings on that day's cricket. In the first he relates how 'the ball lobbed up off Fletcher's boot to forward short-leg, where Intikhab dived and caught it left-handed. It seemed to be news to Fletcher that he had hit it, but Saeed (the bowler) gave a brilliantly persuasive performance and the umpire's finger went up.'

Melford adds later: 'Last night the most relevant statistics seemed to concern how many police or troops would be present today. The Commissioner of Lahore has agreed with Mr Ames that, unless they can keep order, the match cannot continue.' Although this was only the first day of the series, and every one of us had enough natural professionalism to want to complete and win every game, personal safety very quickly began to dominate our thoughts as this unhappy tour went from one trouble-spot to another.

The first Test ended drawn, although we got ourselves into terrible trouble during the second innings and lost our first 5 wickets for only 68. I then played the most important innings of my career to that point, batting four hours for 83 and putting on half-century stands with both Alan Knott and David Brown. Pakistan were left to make 323 in five hours and declined an improbable target after losing three early wickets.

While this match had been taking its unpleasant course, Les Ames had been in constant touch with officials of the Pakistani and British governments, as well as the cricket authorities of both countries. It was now being suggested that we should go on to Dacca for the second Test, even though we were led to understand that the position there had worsened rather than improved. The debate was long and complicated, and when consulted, the players made it quite plain that they were not keen to go.

Our preferences counted for nothing. We went, virtually on the insistence of our Foreign Office, who apparently feared recriminations against the English population of Dacca if we pulled out. We were no longer cricketers, it seemed, but ambassadors being paid a tour fee to keep the peace. It created a great deal of bad feeling and by this stage many of the squad members were muttering that they wanted to go home.

We were assured by soothing political tones that we were in no danger and the match would pass off peacefully if we behaved quite naturally, but our spirits nosedived on arriving in what is now the Bangladeshi capital. The High Commissioner, whose name was Fox, gave the traditional cocktail party to celebrate the team's presence, and it was timed for 6.30 in the evening. Soon after 7 p.m., we were ushered out, without explanation. Most of us were surprised, as these functions invariably occupy a couple of hours, but nobody would have felt offended if we had not met another group of white faces on the way into the building. They turned out to be the representatives of the British and European community, and their purpose in being there was to discuss plans for evacuation!

The entire city was under student law. There was no evidence of policemen, and no troops. The students supervised the traffic and policed the ground when the game got under way. I must say they did a far better job than the police had managed in Lahore and, although the crowds were bigger, the Dacca Test was the most peaceful we played. Peaceful is a relative term in Pakistan, however, and even in Dacca, fighting in sections of the crowd was virtually a constant sideshow, wooden chairs being the favourite weapons of the brawlers.

We realized that the anger of the crowd had little to do with us. They directed most of their abuse against the Pakistani team and against the various politicians trying vainly to run the country. A Test match was simply a convenient stage to protest over much wider issues. Sport, once again, was being dragged into the gutter by politics, and it sickened me to see it happen. We also knew, of course, that patriotism would still have its say; we were not popular, for reasons unconnected with cricket again, and it seemed obvious that any likely English win would be the cue for a severe disturbance. It was not a comforting thought.

One of the few occasions on the tour when tension was lifted came with the arrival of Colin Milburn, who flew to Dacca to reinforce our injury-hit squad. Ollie's omission from the original side was a controversial matter and caused a fair bit of resentment among his growing band of supporters. He had played in two Tests against the Australians the previous summer and, although not a classic opener in the common mould like the adhesive figure of Boycott, he was a great improviser and entertainer. He was also a thoroughly good bloke and a very amusing character. Never had he been needed more urgently.

We decided Ollie should be greeted in style, so the entire squad welcomed him off the plane and escorted him to his hotel, or what we told him was his hotel. In fact, we had booked him into an awful place, just down the road from our own Intercontinental Hotel. We placated him with apologies and explanations that our hotel was full, and then left him to the dirt and the rats. An hour later, we returned to collect him, and took him back to our own hotel. As usual, Ollie took it all in good

46

humour, and he turned out to be a boon for the team both on and off the field.

Pushed straight into the Test side at Karachi, Milburn made a brilliant 139, his best score in Test cricket. Tom Graveney also scored a century and we might in ordinary circumstances have been delighted with our total of 412 for 6. But the rioters were not yet through with us. Both Milburn and Graveney were mobbed on reaching their hundreds, and it was not the type of backslapping which can normally be tolerated. These pitch invaders did not mind whether they slapped you on the back or kicked you on the shin.

I was batting with Tom when he reached his hundred and the scene was appalling. Hundreds of youths came over the fence and headed towards him. The police beat them back, but were then set upon by sections of the crowd, who threw chairs, stones, fruit and anything else they could lay their hands upon. As Tom walked across in an effort to calm them, hundreds more eluded the police cordon and sprinted for the middle. We both gave up at this point, and I think I beat Tom back to the pavilion by a short-head in a race conducted at a good gallop.

Six times in the opening two days, the mob invaded. It was becoming increasingly obvious that the game, and with it the tour, had a limited life. The cricket was meaningless, and we were by this stage concerned with little more than a safe passage home. In the city itself shots were being fired through the night, and it was not the first time on this nightmare trip that this sound had kept us awake. In Lahore, a few weeks earlier, we had been confined to our hotel for a fortnight – a good hotel, with comfortable rooms, a pool and even a small golf course, but now also a boarded-up hotel, guarded day and night by intense-looking men with bren guns. As we could never go out, we had hardly managed any practice at all.

But Karachi, I think, was the most frightening place. We felt under severe threat throughout our stay there, because we knew the students believed they could profit from national press coverage of their disruptions. We had no means of knowing just how far they were prepared to go.

That city gave me my first view of a full-scale operation by riot police. Heaven knows what would have happened if they had waited any longer, because this time the mob was totally out of control. It had begun as a bit of a laugh for us. Alan Knott and David Brown were batting, and little Mushtaq was wheeling away with his leg-breaks. Another disturbance seemed inevitable, just a matter of waiting, and it came as Mushtaq turned to come in for another ball. 'Brownie' had seen the mob coming, but the bowler hadn't, and as he brought back his arm and reached his delivery stride, he was visibly amazed to find he was bowling at unguarded stumps. Both batsmen were by this time sprinting for the relative haven of the pavilion; Mushtaq, as soon as he had familiarized himself with the state of play, followed rapidly.

This time we were not even safe in our dressing-rooms. There were thousands of berserk hooligans streaming across the ground, digging up the pitch and breaking down doors and gates. Then the riot police moved in. Dressed all in blue, and twenty-deep, they started at one end of the ground and moved at a sedate pace into the mob. No one stood in their way, and eventually a degree of sanity was restored, though at what cost I could not say. It was the closest thing I have ever seen to a battlefield on a sports ground, and we knew then that we would be getting out as fast as possible.

Colin Cowdrey was already back in London. He had flown home at the end of the second day's play after a call from his wife had told him of the death of his father-in-law. Everyone sympathized with him over this bereavement, but privately wished they could be going on that plane with him.

To be frank, Cowdrey's leadership had not been strong throughout the troubles. But for the strength and good sense of manager Les Ames, the squad would have been short of leadership. I felt Cowdrey was affected as badly as any of us by the problems. I am not claiming I would have enjoyed the responsibility of captaining a team in

such difficult circumstances, but I was still a little disappointed in him.

Graveney took over for what turned out to be the last
rites of the tour. Following that final, fearful riot, Les
Ames decided that enough was enough and we could stay
no longer to be so abused. By now it seemed that every
player had passed his tolerance level and wanted nothing
further to do with Pakistan.

The most precarious part of it all was still to come,
however, as we now had to be smuggled from the ground
to the airport and out of the country, without alerting the
students to the fact that we were quitting. No one was in
any doubt that our escape plan, once discovered, would
have led to the mob turning all its fury against us
personally.

For reasons of swiftness and comfort, not to mention
the fact that it might mislead 'the enemy', we abandoned
all our gear in the changing-room and took only our
personal belongings with us. On the bus to the airport we
were instructed to keep our heads down, and once into
the terminal we were rushed through all the formalities
and on to a midnight British Airways flight heading home.
None of us, I imagine, has ever been so glad to step on
board a plane and see the smiles of British stewardesses.

My feelings on Pakistan had not altered four years
later. Time may have assuaged some of the bad memories,
but the prospect of having to go there still hung over the
winter like a cloud, which was a great pity as the split
tour began with ten enjoyable weeks in India. Having to
play eight Test matches, in wildly varying conditions,
seemed too much to ask of any touring side in a single
winter, and that trip hopefully spelled the end of such
schedules for ever.

India had been a delight. Even up-country, in some
primitive places where the food and accommodation
leaves plenty to be desired, the country is difficult to
dislike, because every one of the local inhabitants makes
such a visibly determined effort to help. With Tony Lewis
as captain, the spirit of the side remained indomitably
high anyway, and the fact that we lost the series 2–1 was

by no means a disgrace; India, as we have so often found, are extremely difficult to beat on their own territory and, on this occasion, they had four magical spinners at the very peak of their powers and we were without three key players in Ray Illingworth, Geoff Boycott and John Snow. They had each opted not to go, a decision which created something of a stir at the time but, quite properly in my view, was not held against any of them when it came to picking teams the following summer. My own view on this thorny topic is that any player has the right to say he has had enough top cricket and wants a break; it should never prevent a country pursuing the policy of selecting the best available men at all times.

This sector of the tour was especially memorable for me as it provided my maiden Test hundred – a tremendous relief after a wretched start which saw me score only 23 runs in my first four Test innings of the trip. I made only one score of less than 50 in the rest of the series, and finished it with 113 in Bombay out of a stand worth 254 with Tony Greig, who was also passing 100 for England for the first time. It is not difficult to imagine my feelings, particularly as the selectors had made no attempt to disguise their view that this tour represented my 'last chance' to establish myself as an England batsman.

But if India was pleasantly memorable, Pakistan once again was unpleasantly difficult to forget. It was the fourth time I had been there and I made up my mind it was also to be my last.

Hyderabad, a town in the Sind desert, staged a Test match for the first time and none of us who played will ever forget it. The ground was dreadful – an outfield of rolled sand which was whipped up by each shot of any power into a stinging sandstorm. The temperature during daylight hours never fell below 100 degrees and many of us suffered sunburn from the heat bouncing back off the pitch. I spent most of the game fielding at slip, and both Alan Knott and myself ended each day with our eyes swollen and sore.

Dennis Amiss handled the situation best of all – he made 100 on the first day and then retired to his bed for most of the rest of the match! 'Sacker', whom I liked enormously on the several tours we undertook together, did seem to make a happy habit of this syndrome, but never was it so marked as in Hyderabad. The rest of us would stagger back into the hotel with cracked lips and on the verge of sunstroke, and Dennis would be in his usual pose, propped up in bed with a good novel and a pot of tea. His penance was a duck in the second innings.

Pakistan appeared to play cricket as a game intended purely for batsmen – rather as India were to do nine years later, when I returned as captain. In this, Pakistan were well qualified to succeed, as they had a batting line-up which included Sadiq, Majid, Mushtaq, Asif Iqbal and Zaheer, not to mention the avuncular but very effective Intikhab, who caused most of the Hyderabad sandstorms with a spectacular innings of 138.

The attitude of Pakistani people towards us had, if anything, deteriorated still further in the four years since our last visit. The Indo-Pakistani war had plainly not helped matters, and the British support for India was openly resented by many people we met; their frustrations were vented on us.

In Lahore we walked into one of the city's major hotels, for an evening meal during the first Test, and the restaurant staff immediately walked out. Then in Hyderabad our base was the grubby Sanges Hotel, where the owner and the chef had been involved in a stabbing incident shortly before our arrival. When the police moved in and removed all the witnesses, there was no one left to run the place and nobody willing to help. Finally, we were saved from what could have been a particularly unpleasant stay by the generosity of the Canadian Embassy staff, who tended to most of our needs and ensured that we did not go hungry.

The inevitable riots were all saved up for the final Test. Karachi again, and this time the first and third days were scarred by the usual insane invasions, and violent confrontations between spectators and policemen bearing rifles and sticks. This game, too, was abandoned, though the crowd was not to blame. It was a dust-storm, whipped up by a stiff breeze, which made cricket impossible on the final evening. What an appropriate way to finish!

6

Ashes and Clashes

The Ashes win in Australia during the winter of 1970–1 was a triumph for captain Ray Illingworth and is still rated among the finest achievements by an England side in recent times. But Fletcher, for whom this was a fraught first tour of Australia, reveals that behind the veneer of success on the field, the principals of the squad were involved in frequent internal bickerings which created an uncomfortable atmosphere.

Every schoolboy with an ounce of interest in cricket knows about the Ashes. To play a part in winning them is the ultimate fantasy of the cricket-lover and while I grew up in Cambridgeshire I know I created 101 Ashes battles in the back garden or on the playing fields. You would think, then, that to actually live out that fantasy and bring home the Ashes would provide me with some of the best memories of my career. But I recall that series of 1970–1 only as a difficult winter scarred by personality clashes.

The problems arose through the captaincy. Ray Illingworth had it, Colin Cowdrey wanted it, and the two – already far removed in terms of background and lifestyle – barely shared a word during the long and arduous seven-Test tour. It ended with Illingworth being hailed as a hero and Cowdrey being almost ignored, but few people outside the team itself knew quite how awkward the affair became.

For background, it is necessary to go back a couple of years to 1969. Cowdrey was the incumbent captain after the ill-fated series in Pakistan, but when injury ruled him out of the six Test matches that summer, Illingworth was recruited. Most people imagined he was there as a stop-gap, but on proving himself a very capable leader, he in fact ensured that Cowdrey never led England again.

There was no overseas tour the following winter, and the South Africans were scheduled to visit England in 1970. I spent the off-season at home, and kept fit by playing football every Sunday morning. Gradually, however, I began to realize I was a marked man, a prize for any hacker with a hangover, and after being chopped down one morning at Stebbing, I gave up the game for good.

That foul, still more annoying as I was homing in on goal, left me with a tiny bone out of place in my shoulder. I later discovered that it could have been put back if I had gone to a hospital immediately, but that I was now stuck with it in its new position. It was very painful for a time, and I could barely move it at all for two weeks, but the worst problem was when I returned to the indoor nets in March, in readiness for the new season. I found that my timing was awry, and I had to work hard to adjust my batting. It was mystifying at first, but the Essex physio told me that the dropping of the shoulder joint meant that my right arm was now fractionally longer than my left.

By now, I was suffering problems of a different nature, and in this I was not alone. The impending arrival of the South Africans had stirred the anti-apartheid demonstrators to one of their most forceful protests, and I was one of a number of England players to receive anonymous letters threatening violence against myself and my family and calling me a 'bastard' for playing against the all-white tourists.

I did not exactly walk around in fear of my life, but I could see that the future of this tour was probably short-lived. It was no surprise when the respective authorities agreed on cancellation, and a five-Test tour by a Rest of the World team was substituted.

Over the years there has been a number of attempts to put together a model World team, but none has been as successful as this venture. The squad, captained by Gary

Sobers, was genuinely representative of the best players available and, ironically, included the biggest names from South Africa. Big crowds watched every match, and England were beaten 4–1, though it must be doubtful whether many stronger sides have ever visited these shores.

I was not chosen for the first game at Lord's, but in the second, at Trent Bridge, I made runs in the second innings and was at the crease with Brian Luckhurst when we completed our only victory of the series. I finished the summer with an average of almost 50 and particularly remember scoring 63 at Headingley, for the reason that Sue gave birth to our first child, Tara, while I was batting.

Sobers was outstanding throughout this series. He scored more runs and took more wickets than any player on either side, and so what he lacked as a captain in tactical awareness was more than compensated for by his rich personal example. Others were less striking: Graeme Pollock had a poor series before making a century in the last game at the Oval and seemed consistently to be undone by the ball drifting into him, often from Basil d'Oliveira. Graeme's brother Peter looked over the hill as a fast bowler; and Barry Richards, although averaging close to 40, seldom showed the brilliance we came to expect from him in the ensuing years of county cricket for Hampshire.

Debates raged for years afterwards over the official status of that series and eventually it was decided that the matches did not merit being included as Tests. To me, this was wrong. I know the England side treated them as Test matches, and there was certainly no shortage of serious intent among the World players. The natural edge of a Test was apparent in every game.

Cowdrey played in four of the games, but Illingworth remained as captain and surprised the many pundits who wrote him off as a player not good enough for the Australian trip by averaging more than 50 with the bat and taking his share of wickets. It was at this point that David Clark was appointed manager of the winter tour party.

My assumption is that Clark got the job because those in power believed Cowdrey would skipper the tour.

Together, they might have made a happy partnership, being of like mind and type. But Clark-and-Illingworth was a fated relationship, and hardly a week went by on the tour without them disagreeing over something. Illingworth was a very strong character and, so far as the players were concerned, he ran the team, but in such an atmosphere it is slightly surprising we achieved such success.

Australia, however, were a weak side that winter. Bill Lawry was still their captain, but approaching the end of his career as an opener and leading a side which lacked punch with the ball. We had John Snow, fast and mean and at the very peak of his career. They had no one in the same league.

Graham McKenzie had been a fine new-ball bowler, but needed a partner with real pace, and the experiments to find one threw up a number of names. Included among them, for the last two Tests of the series, was one D. K. Lillee, young and raw yet already good enough to suggest he would be around on the scene for some years to come.

But Snow was the real difference between the sides. He decided the fourth Test in Sydney with figures of 7 for 40, putting us 1–0 ahead, and the Aussie batsmen never came to terms with his class. Quite apart from being quick, he also moved the ball around off the seam and made it bounce awkwardly from a decent length. No one else could do the same.

Snow was the strike weapon and Geoff Boycott was the batsman around which we built. He had a great series, almost invariably giving us a sound and sensible start. But I am afraid he was as single-minded an individual then as he was a dozen years later. The conflict between Boycott and Illingworth is nothing new – it simmered throughout that tour, occasionally boiling over. The worst came during the match against South Australia state at Adelaide which opened the tour.

It was the usual flat Adelaide pitch, full of runs, and when Illingworth won the toss we all looked forward to some batting practice. Boycott played well, very well in fact, but when he passed his hundred around teatime, a message was sent out from the captain, asking him to

56

either retire or give his wicket away as there were several
others who needed an innings. Boycott would do neither,
and batted on to the close, by which time he had made
173 not out and we were 326 for two. Illingworth was
furious and a major argument ensued, Boycott claiming
that he should be allowed as much time in the middle as
possible at this stage of the trip, and Illingworth count-
ering that the needs of the side came first and accusing
his fellow Yorkshireman of being selfish.

The captain eventually insisted on making his point
and Boycott was out the following morning without ad-
ding to his score. Barry Richards, who was spending a
lucrative winter earning a dollar a run for South Australia, then made himself $224 at our expense and the
state side broke all kinds of records in piling up more
than 600. So, all things considered, it was hardly the
happiest of launches to the tour.

The first two Tests were drawn and the third, scheduled
for Melbourne over the Christmas period, was totally
washed out by some of the worst weather I have ever seen
in an Australian summer. This created another of the
tour's upsets because the six-Test series was now suddenly
increased to seven, with an extra match being inserted to
make up for the lost revenue from Melbourne. This, no
doubt, had been agreed by David Clark after consul-
tations with the Australian officials who were naturally
anxious to recoup losses. But Illingworth was fuming
because, he said, he had not even been consulted on the
matter. As a captain, Ray was concerned primarily for
the players – indeed, he was always a very strong cam-
paigner for the players' rights and comforts – and he
considered we should not be asked to play yet another
high-pressure Test in an already arduous tour. Although
most of the team was behind him, thoroughly unim-
pressed with the imposition, the decision had already been
taken and we had to abide by it, but it certainly did
nothing to help the relationship between captain and
manager.

Illingworth could be bloody-minded, and wanted
things done his way without exception. But he seemed to

me a far more professional captain than Cowdrey had ever been, and I found myself supporting the Yorkshireman's cause. At times he was one-eyed, and that single eye could be a negative one. He accepted victory if it was obviously on but rarely gambled, and his priority generally seemed to be making certain Australia could not win. In Adelaide, the fifth of the seven Tests, we should have gone 2–0 up, but a commanding position was sacrificed when Illingworth decided not to enforce the follow-on. Australia gratefully scrambled out of trouble and the series lived a little longer than might have been necessary.

I had noticed by this stage the Australian habit of backing their winners and deserting their losers. The crowds were poor for the last few Tests of the rubber because England were proving themselves superior, yet four years later, when the roles were dramatically reversed by Lillee and Jeff Thompson, tickets were like gold-dust. I know everyone would rather watch their team win, but this does seem to apply to Australians rather more than other nations. The Indians, for instance, will turn out in their thousands for a Test series no matter what the balance of power may be.

Unlike many cricketers, I never developed a great affection for Australia or its people, though I am prepared to concede that much of my indifference is probably caused by the restraints of a cricket tour. We never have the time to enjoy a real sight of the country or the rural population. Our flitting from city to city brings us into contact only with other cricketers and with people in hotels and bars, and many of the latter give the impression of wanting to start a pointless argument over the relative merits of cricket nations. I grew to realize it was asking for trouble to go into the city-centre bars in Australia, and confined my socializing to the hotel and to organized parties.

But, as I have hinted, our problems in 1971 stemmed much more from our own personnel than from the Australian public. It became increasingly obvious to me that Cowdrey and Illingworth would never settle their differences during the tour. They were total opposites, and now there was the added needle between them of the captaincy issue.

Their antipathy created two camps, a most unhealthy situation for any tour team. There were those who sympathized with Cowdrey and believed him to be the rightful leader and the wounded party, and those who followed Illingworth as the appointed captain and the stronger character. If I was closer to Illingworth, it was because I preferred the way in which he played the game. Cowdrey, to my mind, inspired his own side in no way other than by his personal contribution with the bat. Illingworth had a clear ability to lead and I believe he should have been in charge of the side longer than he was. He looked after the players' interests off the field, but once a game was under way he could be stern and tough with us. He knew, quite simply, how to go about winning at Test cricket.

Cowdrey's form disintegrated during the trip and I believe it was entirely due to his unhappiness at being overlooked for the captaincy. At his age, and his high level of ability, he needed a personal motivation to do well in a Test series, and playing under Illingworth seemed a deterrent rather than a spur. He seldom mixed with the team and appeared to be thoroughly morose towards the end of the trip. He was left out of the Test side and it seemed unlikely he would find his way back. I feel it had been a mistake to select him under Illingworth.

The lowest point for Cowdrey came during the re-arranged Melbourne Test. He managed a total of 13 runs and even his normally sure slip catching deserted him and he put down no less than five chances. Amid newspaper talk of 'Cowdrey's broken spirit', I was recalled to the team at his expense for the Adelaide match – and I had a broken bone in my hand! I did not, it is true, know it at the time. I had been hit at Newcastle, shortly after completing a century against the New South Wales Country XI. Doctors X-rayed the injury and could find no break, so diagnosed strained tendons and put the arm in plaster from the elbow down. I was told it would need a fortnight's rest, which effectively ruled me out of both the Melbourne and Adelaide Tests. Three days later, I went to see a specialist, and he gave a conflicting diagnosis, removed the plaster and injected the ligaments with cortisone. I still missed the Melbourne match, but it was decided I should play in Adelaide with the assistance of pain-killing injections.

It was a bizarre experience. At number three in the order, I sat padded up in the dressing-room, two needles on the table next to me. As soon as the first wicket fell, Bernard Thomas picked up one of the needles and injected my wrist, I picked up the other and injected the knuckle. Then, with the official two-minute limit between batsmen very close, I scrambled down the steps to bat. I was fortunate that the first wicket had been controversial, Boycott being given run-out, and there was a short delay while he threw down his bat, Greg Chappell gave it back with some sharp advice, and Ian Chappell gestured Geoff to leave the field. By the time he finally stalked off, my treatment was just about concluded.

The injections were effective for no more than a couple of hours, so I had to have another at the next interval, but although I was in some discomfort I cashed in on a perfect pitch and made my best score of the series.

It was two months later that I discovered the truth. The arm was still painful when I returned to England, so I visited another specialist, further X-rays were taken and, this time, a long, slim fracture showed up clearly on the plate. An operation was considered, but I settled for three weeks of complete rest and returned in time to start the new home season. Unfortunately, my form did not return so quickly. The Australian series had not been a successful one for me, and now, not for the first or last time, I was discarded by the England selectors.

7

Bounced Around the World

Time after time, Fletcher looked to be establishing himself as an England player, only to be shown the door again after another lean patch. Throughout the early seventies he was an enigma, seldom allowing his Test average to fall below a healthy 40, yet unsure from one week to the next whether he would be batting before a full house for England or a few hundred hardy souls for Essex. In 1973 he was at last hailed as 'arrived' after a match-saving 173 against New Zealand, just as the Kiwis were threatening a first-ever win over England. Fletcher, looking ready to fill the vacancy left by Ken Barrington, then went on the two tours captained by Mike Denness – the extraordinary 1974 trip to the West Indies, and the harrowing battle with Australian pace, twelve months later. This last trip was to leave Fletcher branded as weak against quick bowling, an allegation which riles him even now.

These should have been his peak years, his late 20s with a stack of experience already banked. But instead, his career yo-yoed crazily.

My faith in human nature has been tested on countless occasions over the years. To be honest, I never once felt secure as an England player. No matter how recent my last hundred, the axe seemed permanently poised over me. I was not alone in this, and batsmen seemed to come and go from the Test side with indecent regularity during the early seventies. A decade on, things have changed; players are given the confidence of a few matches in the side and know that stringing together two or three low scores does not automatically lead to rejection. Allan

Lamb in 1982 was a prime example; the selectors recognized his ability and excused a run of failures.

Following the Ashes win in Australia under Ray Illingworth, I was very much an England standby for the next two years, called upon only when the options seemed slim. I played once against India in 1971 and once against the 1972 Australians. Ironically, this second recall was at Headingley, where I had made my unforgettable début four years earlier. This one was a little less acrimonious; I had reached the stage where the attitude of Yorkshire crowds, or any other crowds, could never bother me. I was just pleased to be back, although after that one game, a victory, I was out in the cold again.

It was on the tour of India that winter, and during the home summer which followed, that I began to feel more like a regular, for the first and only time. I played in all six Tests in the summer of 1973 and it was my most successful season for England. At Lord's we were on the brink of being humiliated by Bev Congdon's under-rated New Zealanders, who had piled up a first-innings lead of almost 300, then worked through our batting on the final day.

With two hours remaining, we were only 70 ahead, with 8 wickets down. Geoff Arnold, coming in at number ten, looked precarious and had already given one chance when I decided the only way out was a counter-attack. I had just passed my hundred and Vic Pollard, the stocky off-spinner, was engaged in a profitable spell, with two wickets already to his credit. He was my target.

First I came down the pitch to him and on-drove for 4. Then I followed up with 2 sixes over mid-wicket into the Tavern stand, hitting with the spin, but taking risks, risks I thought necessary. Suddenly, we were 87 ahead, time on our side, pressure mounting on the Kiwis. 'Horse' Arnold grew in confidence and hung around until the end, as it turned out, and I had made 173 when I got out, playing a tired sort of stroke to mid-wicket, just before New Zealand called it a day.

Much was made of the fact that I had batted with a cracked finger. In fact, I had been batting with it all season, and it had scarcely affected me at all. Where I did suffer was in the field, and I am afraid a couple of catches went down, at Test level, which I might otherwise have hung on to.

That century not only gave me confidence, publicity, and the virtual guarantee of a place for the rest of the summer; it also helped put straight my Test record on home soil. Up to that day, I had made only 130 runs in 12 innings in England, and it was not a record I could be proud of. For some inexplicable reason, I had always done better overseas – perhaps because the togetherness of the squad, and its size, meant that I did not feel under such constant pressure to make runs in order to hold down a place. But the fact remained that home-based cricket followers had never actually seen me play a big innings until that late June day in 1973. Before the summer was out, I was to play one or two more.

I made 81 in the last of the three Tests against New Zealand as we won by an innings. From then on, things were bound to get tougher. Next on stage against us were the West Indies, with as powerful a middle order as any I have ever encountered – Kanhai, Clive Lloyd, Kallicharran and Sobers, the first a brilliant and unpredictable right-hander followed by three of the most prolific left-handers in Test history.

Their bowling, generally underestimated, turned out to be almost as potent a force, led by my Essex team-mate Keith Boyce. Now 'Boycey' was a very fine county cricketer, make no mistake, but I never saw him bowl as fast and furiously as he did in that series. He took 19 wickets in the three Tests, the main difference between the sides – and he even made a big score at number nine, just when it seemed we could dismiss them for a reasonable score in the first Test.

Of course, I was no stranger to this man's talent with the bat. I vividly recall a county match at Chelmsford the previous season, when my 'favourite' opponents Yorkshire had left us an improbable target and by teatime on the final day the draw seemed inevitable. Or it would have been if the opposition had been anyone else. Brian Taylor told us to make sure of the draw, as to carry on chasing runs would only lead to defeat, but this was one occasion where I was happy to disobey orders. Boycey and I were batting, and we told Brian that we meant to carry on trying to win.

The turning point was provided by Richard Hutton. Known as 'Archie' by the Yorkshire side, Hutton was an amusing character off the field, and could be great company. On the MCC Under-25 tour to Pakistan some years earlier he had shown his eccentric side by carrying an army overcoat with him wherever we went. His father, apparently, had told him he would need it for the chilly evenings, but in fact it was not until our final stop that he ever needed to put it on. Like so many others, though, 'Archie' changes dramatically when you put a ball in his hand and tell him to bowl. He was a genuinely nice bloke but one of the most aggressive on the county circuit, constantly berating and insulting batsmen who dared to play him through gully off a thick edge or, sin of sins, miss outside off stump. Against Boycey he went too far, and the abuse directed down the wicket made our West Indian grind his teeth and bat like a whirlwind.

We had needed 154 from the last 20 overs, but with Boyce throwing the bat, and a few shots coming from the other end, too, we got home with something to spare and Hutton finished with nought-for-plenty. Another satisfying notch against the Yorkies.

That was Boyce with the bat. My problem, in the 1973 series, was Boyce with the ball. I did have one or two advantages over the other England players in that I had played with him so often over the years that I knew intuitively each time he was going to bowl a quicker ball, and I was often able to adjust accordingly. All the great quick bowlers have these subtle changes of pace and, when they really let go, the delivery is virtually certain to be either short, or of yorker length. If the batsman knows it is coming, it cuts down the options he has to plan for.

Geoff Boycott was one of the few to play Boyce with any assurance in the first Test at the Oval, where he took 11 wickets. He was no real threat in the next game at

The family man. Keith Fletcher at home in sleepy Great
Easton, with wife Sue and daughters Sarah (left) and Tara

Right: Early days — in the nets at Caldecote, and in Saturday best for a village match

Below: While still a teenager Fletcher showed enough ability to be talked about in Test terms. Here he pulls confidently during an Essex match against the West Indies in 1966

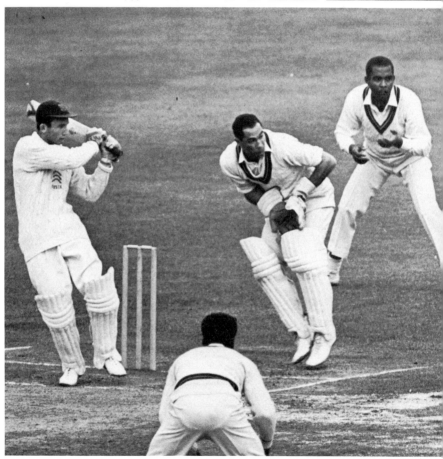

Top: The men with whom Fletcher grew up in county cricket. Trevor Bailey (centre, front row) was about to retire from the captaincy and hand over to Brian 'Tonker' Taylor (far right, front row)

Above: England's team against the Rest of the World, at Lord's in 1970. Ray Illingworth and Colin Cowdrey are front-row neighbours, but were destined not to feel so close during the following winter's Australian tour

Above: A collector's item picture . . . but Keith's leg-spin has
in fact brought him almost 50 first-class wickets

Facing page: Four men central to Fletcher's story — Basil
d'Oliveira (top left), unwitting cause of the South African
storm, Ray Illingworth (top right), tough Yorkshireman but
master captain, Bob Willis (bottom left), Fletcher's shock
successor as England captain, and Raman Subba Row
(bottom right), manager of the 1981−2 tour to India

The men who won the 1980 Championship, gathered at
pre-season training

At last, the Championship! The 1980 triumph is
celebrated by Messrs Smith, Turner, East, Acfield, Denness
and Hardie after the Duke of Edinburgh's presentation to
Fletcher

Birmingham, but at Lord's, with the West Indies 1-up, he seemed to find another gear again. Bowling at a hostile speed, he took 4 wickets in the first innings and was racing in again in the second, as we followed on in disarray, more than 400 runs behind.

Dennis Amiss fell early, which brought in Brian Luckhurst to join Boycott for the closing overs. Luckhurst had been caught behind off Boyce early on in the first innings, and clearly did not much fancy the prospect of him, so with the last over looming up, I gather the conversation in mid-wicket consisted of a request from the Kent man to his Yorkshire team-mate to take Boyce's last fling, followed by an angry retort from the Yorkshireman.

I have not always sympathized with Boycott, but here I was in full agreement with him. Luckhurst was a recognized opener for his county and, with the shine off the ball anyway, it seemed unfair that he should pass the buck to Boycott just because he was not confident against Boyce. I have never asked anyone to shield me from the strike, and I hope I never have to.

The upshot was an unprofessional reaction from Boycott, who fell straight into Boyce's trap and hooked the short ball to Kallicharran, deep at square leg. He claimed angrily in the dressing-room that Luckhurst was to blame for ruining his concentration, but both men took a rocket from Ray Illingworth.

It was a fiery day in more than one respect, for this was the Saturday when Lord's was subjected to a bomb scare. The IRA's evil campaign was centred on London at the time, and the authorities wisely decided that the telephone threat could not be ignored, whatever the odds on it being a hoax by some misguided crank. The crowd was asked to leave and the West Indian players returned to their hotel, while we waited in a tent behind the pavilion. With the search completed, and the all-clear given, play was able to resume – so maybe it was a little more than Luckhurst's buck-passing that disturbed Geoffrey's concentration.

Our cause was lost, anyway, and with two days left the most we could hope for was to extend the game as long as possible and regain some respect. This was partially achieved, although it was still over by mid-afternoon on the Monday. I finished unbeaten on 86, having top-scored in both innings, and in such desperately unbalanced circumstances I still regard that as one of my best achievements for England.

If nothing else, it ensured that I would be on the flight to the Caribbean in January for what promised to be a daunting tour. If we had been so convincingly beaten by the West Indies on our own patch, one hesitated to contemplate the possible outcome on wickets they knew and weather they revelled in. Moreover, the era of Ray Illingworth's captaincy had come to an inglorious end, and the selectors had turned to a man who had not been thought good enough to play a single Test during the summer just ended.

I did not know Mike Denness particularly well at the time. In subsequent years, we became close, both through shared experiences with England and the fact that he left Kent to spend the closing years of his county career under my captaincy at Essex. I grew to like him, and I think he will agree that he mellowed, becoming a more relaxed and agreeable person. But in the West Indies, and a year later in Australia, he was under such pressure from so many sources that it would have needed a quite extraordinary constitution to even appear relaxed. Here was a man who had played nine Tests, and those without rip-roaring success, being asked to undertake the toughest of missions – with his senior player constantly appearing, in the view of many of us, to be trying to undermine his authority.

I refer, of course, to Geoff Boycott. He was 33 at the time, had played fifty-seven Tests and made no secret of the fact that he considered it to be a scandal that he had once more been overlooked for the England captaincy – indeed, even for the vice-captaincy, which had gone to Tony Greig.

Boycott was not alone in questioning Denness's appointment; it was, on paper at least, a surprising selection. But Boycott was the only one who turned it into a personal issue. For much of the tour, I felt he gave Mike little co-operation at times when his experience and knowledge might have been of great benefit. Worse still, he spent some of his time conducting what seemed to me an unofficial campaign to get Denness out.

He came to me one day and put his grievances, suggesting that the senior players should group together and enforce a change in leadership. I thought it was a cynical idea and simply told him that we were in the middle of a series and should concentrate on winning it, putting other considerations to one side until the time was suitable to discuss them.

Considering the background, it says much for Boycott that it was his century, coupled with Tony Greig's off-breaks, which turned the series on its head.

We had been under the cosh almost constantly. We lost the first Test heavily in Port of Spain, and we could almost hear the pundits proclaiming the likelihood of a 5–0 whitewash. To be fair, few of us would have staked our mortgage against it happening. Yet somehow we staged survival shows in each of the next three matches and went into the last Test – again on Trinidad – only 1–0 down after being hopelessly outplayed by a very fine side.

The Port of Spain pitch would turn, we had no doubts about that, and in consequence we packed our side with four spinners – Derek Underwood to bowl his own unique brand of slow left-arm, the specialist off-spinners Pat Pocock and Jack Birkenshaw, and Greig to double up as third offie and a seamer. Of the four, we imagined Greig was the least experienced spinner . . . but then, everything about the match surprised us.

Boycott made 99 in the first innings; Greig then took 8 wickets. Still we trailed by 38 runs. Boycott then improved on his first effort and scored 112 out of 263, but with only 226 runs needed to win, the West Indies remained warm favourites. Greig changed that with another superb spell, angling his off-breaks from round the wicket into the bowlers' rough outside the left-hander's off-stump. As four of the top six West Indians happened to bat left-handed, this caused untold problems, and they collapsed to 199 all out.

It was a wonderful end for us, but it must have sickened the West Indies. Their captain, Rohan Kanhai, had surely been to blame for letting us off the hook so often during the series, when a stronger man would have ground us into the dust.

Boycott's part in the triumph could not be under-estimated, and I must confess I wondered just what he was thinking as we celebrated afterwards; his runs had made it certain that Mike Denness would stay as captain. Boycott's ego was plainly suffering; his relish for Test cricket disintegrated and a few months later he began his three-year exile by announcing himself unavailable for England.

As for Denness, it must be said that he had little help from certain other senior players on that Caribbean trip, but he weathered the worst of the storm and went on to lead the side in the two 1974 home series, a 3–0 win over India and a scoreless draw with Pakistan. Then it was back to sterner business. The Ashes had to be defended in Australia that winter. We already knew all about Lillee and what a menace he could be to us, but none of us had even heard of the other fellow who was to burst on the scene, breathing fire and threatening all kinds of injuries to any batsman who happened to stand in his way. Jeff Thomson was still unknown, but before the tour was over we were all wishing he had stayed that way.

My first brush with him came in the state game against Queensland at Brisbane, and he gave me something to remember him by. We had seen his name bandied around the press by this time; Australians seemed to be pinning their hopes on this raw, rough boy from the beaches teaming up with Dennis Lillee and throttling the life out of the Poms. It gave the Aussies a great kick when Thommo, in one memorable interview, boasted that he enjoyed the sight of batsmen's blood while he was bowling.

The Queensland match was the last before the Test series began. It was also played on a pitch prepared by

Clem Jones, that Brisbane personality who came down from the mayoral chambers and insisted on taking over groundsman duties at the Gabba. He may have been a good mayor, but he did little for that pitch. It was the first of several wickets we were to encounter on this tour which could only be described as dangerous. Brisbane, although lively and underprepared, turned out to be by no means the worst.

It was in our second innings that Thomson wound himself up to full power. I went in with 3 wickets down cheaply, and had not been there long when he pitched only just short of a length and made the ball rear up, smashing me on the left elbow. It was one of the more painful blows I have taken while batting, and I needed a few minutes to recover. But I was determined not to go off; at that stage of an Ashes tour, any signs of weakness are exaggerated in the propaganda war. I stayed for more than an hour, and with great satisfaction saw Thomson out of the attack by hitting him for 4 fours in half a dozen balls. It would have been nice to think that might have been the final word on the matter, but Thomson's bowling had plenty of vocabulary left in it yet. He was to end the series with 33 wickets from five matches, and we were to end it with a 4–1 beating, the single consolation victory coming from a final Test in which both Thomson and Lillee were 'crocked'.

We had nothing to rival them. Bob Willis was our strike bowler, and did the job manfully. But on that tour he was not as quick or dangerous as he was later to become and there was no one of comparable pace to support him. Any fast bowler will be much more effective with a partner, as has been proved on countless occasions over the years.

Our cause was not helped by the sequence of bad pitches on which batting against extreme pace became a nightmare. Many were simply not flat; there were saucepan lids of brown, where the skimming mower had removed the grass, and valleys of green which the mower had missed. This naturally meant the ball bounced at inconsistent heights, and was directly responsible for some literally frightening deliveries.

Thomson left his mark on the first match of the series, taking 9 wickets in Australia's convincing win in Brisbane. But it was at Perth a fortnight later that he bowled one of the most lethal deliveries I have ever faced and convinced me he must rank alongside the quickest of all Test bowlers. I had time only to get my glove in front of my face, and the deflection was travelling so fast that it actually thumped the chest of wicketkeeper Rodney Marsh standing more than 20 yards back, before he got his gloves to it. I was out for 0, to add to my 4 in the first innings. We were well beaten again.

Sydney, venue for the fourth Test, provided us with the worst pitch. When you consider the speed of the bowling we were being asked to face, it was just about the most dangerous surface I have ever seen. One delivery from Dennis Lillee even scared the bowler, who is not known for squeamishness when it comes to intimidation. Geoff Arnold was facing and, if not exactly quaking, I would bet he felt more nervous than usual as Lillee banged one in short. It rose quickly and Arnold, not sighting it in time, threw up his bat with the primary objective of protecting his face. Too late. The ball was through him before he knew it, searing through the tiny gap between bat and head, still rising as it cleared the leaping Marsh and whacking into the sightscreen first bounce. It was small wonder, seeing things like that occur, that our tail-enders expressed an honest reluctance to get into line. With their limited techniques, they were unlikely to last long anyway, and physical injury – or worse – was never far from anyone's mind during this series.

None of us enjoyed going out to bat. I thought of it as my job to get in line, play straight and try to build an innings as naturally as possible. But the knowledge that one needed to move very fast to keep one's body intact was not a pleasant way to spend a day in the sunshine, and there were times for all of us when a few weeks in frozen England seemed quite a palatable alternative to yet another session of ducking the stream of short balls.

At least half a dozen times, I flicked my head out of the way through sheer instinct as balls I had not seen at all whipped past the end of my nose. Some missed me by only fractions of an inch and I am sure that someone unused to quick bowling, or simply someone older with slower reactions, would have been hit on the head.

In the midst of all this, enter Colin Cowdrey. A man whose Test career seemed to have been ended by the previous tour of Australia under Illingworth, was now answering an English SOS following a couple of injuries. He was approaching his 42nd birthday, also close to retirement from the first-class game. Yet he could not resist the final challenge. He was thrown straight into the Test side at Perth, on a fast, bouncy wicket and against an ogre, in Thomson, he had never set eyes upon. What is more, he even opened the second innings, Luckhurst having joined the casualties.

I have no idea how he survived. More than once, I watched him go to hook either Lillee or Thomson, only for Marsh to be holding the ball above his head before Cowdrey was even half-way through with the shot. Sensibly, he scrubbed the stroke off the menu, but the fact remained that he needed more time than the rest of us to adjust. His defensive technique was as sound as ever, though; he got into line and played the ball on its merit, often being struck on the body but never flinching from the job. He made 22 and 40 in that match, as courageous a performance as I have seen in a Test.

Another man returning to Test cricket in Perth was Fred Titmus, and his break had been even longer, since 1968 in fact, when that horrible boating accident in the West Indies left him minus two toes. Somehow he had fought back into the England squad and he, too, showed a good deal of fortitude against the quicks. Not in the classical mould of Cowdrey, for Freddie never did claim to be in that class as a batsmen, but in an obdurate way he had worked out for himself. Fred believed that if he moved quickly across outside off-stump as the ball was bowled, he could easily duck under all the short stuff and still be in line to play anything that was of decent length. He tried this at Perth to great effect, scoring 61 in the second innings while the Aussies scratched their heads

71

trying to work out how to counter his tactics. But in the next match at Melbourne, Lillee found the antidote, coming round the wicket to Titmus, who walked straight into the angled bouncer and had both feet off the ground in confusion as he gloved it to gully, abandoning the scheme at a stroke.

David Lloyd suffered one of the nastiest blows of the tour, when Thomson, making the ball lift viciously from just outside off-stump, hit him squarely in the box with a sickening crunch and almost lifted him over the stumps. It ruined David's confidence for the rest of that tour, and despite batting consistently for Lancashire, he has never played for England since.

Batsmen do get shellshocked in series like this one. I have seen it happen to Dennis Amiss, John Edrich and Geoff Boycott, all fine players. There is no point in pretending an immunity because no one is safe from the psychological problems which inevitably result. The problems begin as soon as you start to wonder if you are quick enough to keep getting out of the way of the short ball. Tailenders get frightened, which is fair enough under the circumstances, but even the leading batsmen are apprehensive.

If you freeze you are certain to get hit. It happened to me once against Thomson, during that unhappy game at Sydney. The ball was short and fast, but I had a reasonable sight of it. For some inexplicable reason, my reactions just did not work in time, and the best I could do was get a glove-edge on to the ball before it struck me in the middle of my cap and looped out towards cover. Ross Edwards skinned his arm as he dived forward in a vain attempt to catch me and I remember thinking rather malevolently that I was glad one of the opposition was suffering as well as us.

Sydney produced one of the flashpoints of the tour, Lillee inevitably being involved. His tolerance threshold always has been low, and when Greig hit him on the elbow with a bouncer, he did not accept that it was a perfectly reasonable return of fire by a frustrated batsman. His bat flew out of his hands as if he had been hit by a

72

delivery of his own pace rather than Greigy's compara-
tively friendly medium. I walked forward from slip to pick
up his bat and held it out to him, saying something only
slightly cutting such as 'Did it hurt?' He went off like a
firecracker, aiming a stream of abuse at me so unexpected
and uncalled for that I threw his bat back on the grass
and walked off, leaving him to pick it up himself.

That might have been the end of it, if the crowd had
allowed. But 50,000 people inside the Sydney ground had
observed all and drawn their own partisan conclusions as
to what was said by us both. When I went out to bat the
following day Lillee was at the end of his run and the
crowd was verging on hysteria, baying 'Kill, Kill, Kill.'
I knew exactly what to expect and was prepared for it.
The first two balls pitched in Lillee's half rather than
mine, and I was ducking virtually before they had left his
hand. The next hour was torrid, but I survived to the
close and saw off the worst of Lillee, finally getting out to
Max Walker the next morning.

The second innings was no friendlier. John Edrich, one
of the bravest, gutsiest players I have ever known, was
struck first ball in the ribs by Lillee. I heard the crack
from the dressing-room, and every one of us knew there
must be a break. I was next in, and can't claim I was
looking forward to it greatly.

Our team spirit had stood up remarkably well considering the beating we were taking, but inevitably the odd
nerve was exposed. Things were made more difficult by
Denness's desperate batting problems. He, more than
anyone else, utterly failed to find his form, and decided
to take the initiative and drop himself for the Sydney
Test, Edrich taking over as captain.

I cannot rate Denness as a great captain, either tactically or inspirationally, and if I sympathized when he was
wrongly crucified for the Edgbaston fiasco later in 1975,
I could not help feeling that he contributed to his own
unhappy position on the tour by failing to listen to well-
intentioned advice. I admit it was not always offered –
and if I am to make a criticism of Edrich it would be for
his reluctance to fully support his skipper – but when it

was, Denness gave the impression that he was already in command and beyond interference. I fear he was not always right in that respect.

Certain players did resent his attitude, and I believe one even got to the stage of considering a refusal to play under Denness, such was his difficulty in communicating with him.

No tour is ever entirely free from personality clashes, particularly a losing tour, but I will say this one was probably a more contented party than the winning squad of four years earlier. It was, to make a trite understatement, only the fast bowlers who separated the teams. Given Lillee and Thomson on our side, we would have won just as convincingly. But the Australians revelled in their few months of glory, and I could not blame them. They had discovered a pair of champion bowlers who, it seemed at the time, might see them through to the next Ashes series in Australia.

Looking back now, I am amazed that no one so much as mentioned the possibility of developing a helmet for use against them. We must all have been mad. There we were, against the quickest partnership for many years, holding rigidly to tradition, when a blow on the temple could have killed any one of us. I remain astonished that it did not happen, and the irony is that death almost did blight the tour – but it was one of our own bowlers, Peter Lever, who administered the blow, to Ewan Chatfield in New Zealand.

I seldom mixed socially with the Australians and hardly got to know Lillee or Thomson. Some players enjoy the socializing with opponents at the end of a day's play, but I cannot bring myself to go and drink with someone who has been trying to knock my head off just a few minutes earlier.

8

The Essex Double

In 1973 Essex won four and drew three of their first seven Championship matches, and stood at the top of the table for virtually the first time in Fletcher's ten years as a capped player. But this, his benefit season, was not destined to be the one to end the long, frustrating wait for honours. It was, however, the end of an era. 'Tonker' Taylor retired at the end of the summer and, to the surprise of nobody, Fletcher was appointed to succeed him.

The germ of Essex's successes in the late seventies had been planted ten years earlier. Although we never won anything under Brian Taylor, the mental approach of the side improved beyond recognition, and the most fundamental reason was the introduction of the John Player League.

I have already related the scandalous way in which we ignored the Gillette Cup in its early years, some of our players considering it a rude intrusion into their free time. We had come some distance since those amateurish days, and with the determination of 'Tonker' inspiring us, we attacked the new Sunday league season with relish.

Brian Taylor may not have had the greatest tactical gifts cricket has seen, but he was both sensible and ambitious, and from the moment that the JPL began, he realized it was potentially our sort of competition. We were a young, fit side – the days when half the team could not bend and would not run in the field had long gone – and we had a bowling attack which was developing on lines which seemed ideal for the needs of this new challenge. We trained specifically for the Sunday league and, for a club of our modest past, we did superbly well to finish second to Lancashire in its opening season in 1969.

For the first time in my career, the public began to take Essex seriously that year. More important still, the players began to believe they were nowhere near as inept as they might be led to believe. There was still a long way to go, but we were on the right road.

'Tonker', to his great credit, had learned from our wasteful attitude to the Gillette. We were not the only county to treat limited-overs cricket as a joke – it seems a remote and unlikely stance now, but many were cynical in those early days. Only Yorkshire, so far as I recall, were openly hostile towards the innovation and to this day I am baffled by their attitude because there is still an element in their club which insists that the one-day game has no place in cricket. They are wrong, horribly wrong, and if they only bother to take off their blinkers and look around they will see for themselves all the good it has done.

I have always enjoyed one-day games, and still do. If not from the start, then very soon afterwards I saw what a boon they were going to be for a game having desperate difficulty in attracting people to the grounds. It was a smack in the eye for tradition – not that that is a bad thing – and it certainly was not cricket as my generation was brought up to play it. But that did not mean it had no valid place in the sport. The public clamour was enough to persuade all right-thinking people that the players should adapt to the change and provide the sort of instant entertainment that spectators clearly wanted to see. Yorkshire were so short-sighted that they could not even see the financial bait before their noses; if they had ever been a successful one-day side, I am convinced they would have had enormous support.

If, however, the sole benefits had been financial, to the detriment of playing standards, I would not have been enthusiastic. The fact is, limited-overs cricket has elevated our fielding standards to a level never before seen in this country, and probably in the world. No teams would succeed if they had to hide three or four slouches; there simply isn't room. So practice, on a previously improbable scale, was the only answer, and in my time at Essex I have seen some initially geriatric customers turned into very adequate fieldsmen by the pressure on their place if they failed.

Every side has learned the art of the one-day game over the years, some, naturally enough, much better than others. Containing bowling was the first advance; pacing an innings rather than slogging indiscriminately was another. From a captain's point of view, field placing became more crucial, bowling changes could be decisive and a switch in the batting order could turn a tight game. It was pressurized sport, and over the years the pressure has intensified as every county has risen to a level of being able to compete. There are few easy games in the one-day competitions now.

Essex, as I say, had moved with the times and when I took over from 'Tonker' in 1974, it was in the limited-overs events that I was most optimistic. Although we had slipped down the John Player League the previous year, we had reached the semi-finals of the Benson and Hedges Cup, which was only two seasons old, and the last eight in the Gillette. Surely our turn would come soon?

I felt I was playing at my peak around that time. In 1973 I had been an established regular for England, almost for the only time in my career, and I had also been named among *Wisden's* five Cricketers of the Year. I remember Trevor Bailey writing of me in *Wisden* that 'the big surprise is not so much that 1973 should see him become an automatic choice for England, but rather that it should have taken him so long to arrive.' What he did not know, and I could only fear, was that I had barely arrived when I was asked to leave again!

The fact that I was often away on Test duty hampered Essex throughout 1974. It was not so much my playing ability that was missed, but the presence and authority of a resident captain. The team drifted; I knew it but was helpless to do anything about it. We dropped to twelfth in the Championship, a dismal fifteenth in the JPL, and made no show in the knockout competitions. Hardly an auspicious start for the new man in charge.

My England experiences did have their uses, though. I had seen at first hand the reaction of international players to winning, and it was an important influence on me. Winning was not a habit yet at Essex. We had not learned to do it, nor developed a belief that it was possible. I picked up hints from people like Brian Close, a warrior-like fighter for England and, when captaining Yorkshire, the type who would bully his players into winning and kick them if they didn't. I tried to instil something similar at Essex, but without the brute force which was so successful for Closey. I worked on our players, individually and as a unit, trying to give them confidence, but it was not something which could bring overnight rewards. We were a developing side; players like Graham Gooch, Ken McEwan and John Lever were still some way short of their peak. In time, I felt sure, we would be a formidable team, and the thought that I could captain Essex to their first honour in a century motivated me more than even the honour of playing for England. These, after all, were the people I lived with day to day, and I desperately wanted to help bring them some success at last.

The indications of progress were apparent in 1975. We made good advances in both the league competitions and as England could not make up their mind whether I was part of their plans or not, I was available for seventeen of Essex's first-class matches, although ironically this co-incided with one of the worst seasons of my career. I failed to reach 1000 runs and did not even make a first-class century. To be honest, I was still not fully enjoying the captaincy role and there were times when I silently wondered if I should carry on with it.

Certain parts of the job were no problem to me. On the field, I felt in adequate control, because I had been involved with the team's tactics for so long, and to do things entirely my own way was a satisfying bonus. But a county captain is expected to contribute very much more than merely leading his team out, setting the fields and changing the bowlers.

The hardest thing then, and even now, was to inform people when they had been left out. Every captain will say the same, I have no doubt. Although most players take it reasonably well, it is an unpleasant feeling to be taking away part of their life, if only temporarily, and I sometimes wondered just what the unlucky ones privately thought about me. With years of experience one becomes hardened and probably even better at breaking bad news, but it is still never easy.

The other duty I found particularly daunting was public speaking. As soon as I was elevated to the captaincy, the demands on my time increased. Although I had been an England player for some while, Essex clubs and societies are naturally keen to have the Essex captain at their functions, so it was only in 1974 that my social diary grew overcrowded and I was assailed too often by the sort of nerves I suppose actors must feel on first nights . . . the difference was that I was suffering from them every night I performed.

I have a vivid, nightmarish memory of the first speech I ever had to make. As usual, I had made an effort to prepare something in advance, but once I had stood up and stared at the eager audience for a moment or two, every idea in my head vanished without trace.

I mumbled pleasantries for a few minutes, probably making little sense and realizing with a jolt just how strange my voice sounded. Then I dried up completely. Just stood there, with nothing more to say Finally, I thanked everyone and sat down again, feeling more embarrassed than I have ever done on being out for 0.

Now, of course, I know just how many people are affected this way by public speaking. There are those who have a natural gift for it, the gregarious and comical types, but there are many more who find it formidably difficult. I have lost count of the amount of times I have sat at a function and squirmed in discomfort for the poor bloke stuttering and stammering through a speech. I could relate to them all more than they ever knew. Even Ray

East, as renowned a character and funny man as exists on the cricket circuit, is a bundle of nerves on these occasions and I have watched him dry up in just the way I did.

Eventually, I began to improve, learning to say a few simple things as clearly as possible, expound one or two views on the game, tell a funny story if I happened to have one, and then sit down again. I realize I will never be in demand as an entertainer, even now, but it was a case of having to perfect a method of blundering through these speeches because they became so frequent. In recent years there have been times when I would have been out every night of the week for most of the winter if I had accepted each invitation offered. I decided I would do no more than two each week unless the circumstances were exceptional and the extra function happened to be for a close friend. Even then, it took a sizable chunk of my free time. Most dinners are held on Friday or Saturday evenings, which meant I was often sacrificing much of my weekend.

Leaving the actual speaking aside, the most difficult part of such functions is to continually summon an acceptable level of enthusiasm. For the members of the club concerned it is often their biggest social gathering of the year and they will be determined to enjoy themselves, which in many cases means getting steadily drunk and falling over on the dance floor. I never wished to seem ungracious or unsociable, but it was impossible for an outsider like myself to enter fully into the spirit of every club's shindig, and I would usually try to slip away before midnight.

Being captain also entailed serving on various county committees, but this was something I enjoyed. I discovered I was getting far more fulfilment out of cricket by being involved in the workings of the club and the decisions which affected the team, and to this day I still serve on the cricket and executive committees and look forward to the meetings. Dealing with the press was another thing which did not disturb me at all. That might sound surprising, knowing my dislike of speaking, but there is a world of difference between giving an interview on cricket to one journalist, or a conference to a dozen, and standing up alone and unassisted to make 100 or 200 people laugh.

These jobs, however, were all secondary in my estimation to the needs of the team and our ambitions to win something. There had been a small inheritance of problems when I took over the side, the thorniest of which was that we had three capped spinners on the staff, none of whom could bat. That is not intended to be unkind, because both Robin Hobbs and Ray East had made valuable runs for the team even if David Acfield was a self-confessed rabbit; but not one of the three had any pretensions to be considered on their merits with the bat and there did not seem the slightest chance that we could keep them all happily employed. I envisaged this becoming a tricky situation, as they were all fine bowlers in their own right, but one of them clearly had to go. My own view was, and still is, that orthodox finger spinners, either right- or left-arm, will win more games in English conditions than a leg-spinner, and although 'Hobbsy' was the best of a dying breed in this country, it was something of a relief to me when he solved the problem by telling me he intended to retire at the end of the 1975 season.

Robin was not only a talented and wholehearted cricketer – he later returned to the game as captain of Glamorgan, so the taste for it had scarcely died – but he was also a very funny man, one of the most comical characters I have ever met in cricket and the chap who really set the pattern for the image Essex have maintained to this day.

He was the forerunner of a chain which continued with Ray East, was taken up by Keith Pont and has since been perpetuated by men who at first seemed improbable humorists, like Graham Gooch and, in the new generation of Essex players, Alan Lilley.

To be honest, everyone in our side can be funny, and it must be a good thing. I can see them develop as personalities by being brought out of themselves. Graham Gooch was extremely quiet when he first came to us. I remember seeing him in our indoor school when he was 12 years old and remarking on how shy he was. Even to the time when he first played for England, in 1975, he was an introverted type and I think if he had played for certain other, less animated teams, he might have turned out rather differently. As it is, he now purveys some inspired, off-the-cuff remarks in the dressing-room and impersonates accents and idiosyncrasies as well as anyone I have seen.

Ray East would be the first name most people would mention if asked for a cricketing character, but his clowning is really only a cover for nerves. Ray is as highly-strung a cricketer as any I have come across, and larking around on the field is his way of camouflaging it. He can be hilarious, because his comic acts have been quite rigorously rehearsed over the years and he has a fine sense of spontaneous absurdity; but just occasionally he has gone too far and then it is only right that the captain should stamp on it. Equally, Ray can go the other way, and from apparently being the colourful, comical centre of attention he retreats into his shell.

In general, humour can relax the side in tight situations and, conversely, it can keep them interested on the boring days which inevitably occur occasionally during a long season. Our jokers range from the vivid humour of East and Gooch to the dry, laconic wit of David Acfield. But nobody ever stoops to vindictive humour, aimed either at each other or opponents. I have experienced it in other dressing-rooms and found it tasteless and divisive.

To my mind the funniest character in our side is Keith Pont. He is a natural wit who does not even have to work hard for his laughs. He started his career the way he meant to go on when, during his début match, he found he was being semaphored by 'Tonker' from third man at one end to third man at the other. We were playing on a park ground and there was a boy's bike lying on the boundary, so Ponty hopped on this and rode around the line to his position for the next over. 'Tonker' took it well and the rest of us were helpless with laughter. A funny man was born that day, and he has not changed a bit since.

If all this merriment suggests that Essex have been an

undisciplined lot over the years then it is misleading. When there is work to be done – and work normally means the winning of a match – then the players under my captaincy have given their all. But relaxation and diversions are essential in the odd life of a county cricketer who is often away from home for a week or more, often works seven days a week but sometimes does very little of an active nature for a day or more. Players can get bored and they will get disillusioned unless they are allowed a certain leeway.

I apply similar discretion to behaviour in the evenings. There is no point in wrapping the players in cotton-wool, pretending they are schoolkids and inflicting curfews. The instinct, quite naturally, will be to rebel.

Cricketers are professional sportsmen, professional entertainers, and as such I expect them to be sensible enough to look after themselves. If they don't, then they won't play in my side. It is as simple as that; everyone knows just how far he can go, and it is up to the individuals whether they want to abuse the system.

In my experience, the Essex players have been very good. I am not going to pretend they have always behaved angelically or that there have not been mornings when hangovers have been obvious at the breakfast table. I can overlook anyone having too much to drink once in a season. But if they go beyond that limit, then I would act.

I am not the greatest advocate of regular team talks but there are occasions when they are necessary. I try to avoid dwelling on the opposition in these instances; in most cases the players against us are familiar and it achieves nothing positive to build up their strengths in the minds of our players. Instead, I like to talk about what we are going to do, and how we propose to win.

On the field, I have always encouraged everyone to chip in with his own thoughts on any particular situation. When I was not captain, Brian Taylor sought my opinion frequently, sometimes acting on it, sometimes not. I try to do the same, and then decide which is good advice and which is rubbish. At least a player who puts forward an idea is thinking about the game, which usually means he is mentally right for the job. I try to instil in youngsters coming into the side that they must think about their cricket; too many, these days, seem content to meander through each season in a semi-daze, thinking no further ahead than the next delivery.

An alert mind is essential, but I don't think that necessarily means devoting complete attention to every delivery when your own side is batting. I watch very little of the play immediately before my own innings, but as soon as the wicket falls I know I am prepared, and I have a complete plan of how I am going to bat. Too many, I suggest, go out with precious few thoughts in their heads at all.

Success crept up on us gradually through the late seventies. Although to outsiders it probably seemed inevitable that we would finish among the honours before long, to us there was a whole series of frustrations to be borne first. The John Player League seemed destined to elude us by the narrowest of margins; we continued to improve in the Championship without quite toppling the likes of Kent and Middlesex, and in the knockout competitions we were forced to settle for second-best from some epic matches. I think particularly of the Gillette semi-final at Taunton in 1978, which remains one of the best limited-overs games in which I have ever taken part.

Somerset had already scored 297 to beat Warwickshire in the first round, then set Glamorgan an impossible target of 331 in the second. They thrashed the favourites Kent in the quarter-final and we were undoubtedly the underdogs before the usual partisan, vocal crowd of about 10,000 in cider-country. Their hero Vivian did not let them down. Richards took 116 off us and Somerset totalled 287 for 6 from their 60 overs. Although Graham Gooch made 61, we always seemed to be just behind the required rate, but I scored 67, Keith Pont batted frantically and well and suddenly we wanted 12 off the last over, then 3 off the last ball, our 10th-wicket pair at the crease. John Lever swung, sprinted and crossed for 2. Neil Smith, our burly Yorkshireman wicketkeeper, raced back for the third but was run out by inches. The scores were

84

tied . . . but we went out on the basis of having lost more wickets.

We were runners-up in the Championship that year and I felt certain we now had a title-winning side. We had lost Keith Boyce, which was tragic, but in his place had come the quiet Dominican Nobby Phillip, who could hit a ball almost as hard and bowl something like as quick. If he was not quite the quality of Boyce he still turned out to be a marvellous team-man and provided the speedy pressure which John Lever needed at the other end. JK had played fifteen Tests by this time but, in county terms, he reached his peak in the years of 1978 and 1979 – 102 wickets the first year, 104 the next. The ball swung for him almost throughout the whole of 1979, and he went from one set of astonishing figures to another as we simply walked off with the Championship.

It had partly been a question of self-belief. After coming so close the previous season, we were all convinced that we were good enough and that if we played even equally well we would not be denied again. There is a way of forming the winning habit, I am sure of that now. I have seen sides so often get themselves in a position from which they should win a game, yet they simply don't know how to turn the screw. It is the most difficult hurdle for any side to overcome – the difference between a middle-of-the-road county team and a confident, successful outfit.

I would have been happy to win anything that year, but the Championship was clearly our top priority. After all, the Essex club was formed in 1876. They had been making vain attempts on the Championship for more than 100 years. I wanted to prove to everyone that we now had the best team Essex had ever seen, and the only way I could do that was by winning the title they had waited for for so long. Even I, however, could never have imagined we would do it so easily.

If John was our trump card – and in two successive matches in June he took a total of 26 wickets – then depth in batting was our greatest strength. Four men topped 1000 runs, and those apart we could call on Gooch, who was often absent with England, Phillip, Stuart Turner,

Pont and East, all of whom made vital runs at various stages. There was not a weak link in the order.

By the middle of June we were 60 points clear of the field, a phenomenal lead. People said we were lucky with the weather, and so we were. What many of them omitted to mention was that we were winning many of our matches inside two days.

It was a heady feeling. The adrenalin pumped in me all year, because we never lost our impetus, and there were still four matches left when we clinched it on a Tuesday afternoon in August. Not, it is true, in the most romantic of settings – it was the Northampton ground, jammed in the middle of red-brick terrace blocks in the Midlands cobblers' town, and there were no more than 1000 people there to see us do it.

Victory there had come easier than had seemed likely. It had been an even game until Northants lost 8 second-innings wickets in the last two hours of the second day. We were left needing only around 200 to win in most of the third day, and we did it comfortably.

Then came an uncomfortable wait in the usually depressing old changing-rooms – high-ceilinged, floor-boarded and cramped. Until we knew for sure that Worcestershire, our closest challengers, had not won their game, the champagne had to stay on ice. The news came via a press man on the pavilion telephone – and then we did celebrate.

I remember thinking that night how nice it would have been to win it a day later, when Chelmsford would have been virtually full for the occasion and Surrey, our neighbours, were the visitors. But then, after waiting 103 years, it might seem churlish to complain about an odd day.

To be strictly chronological, we had already broken our honours duck by that time. In late July we reached and won the Benson and Hedges Cup final and, if the achievement itself cannot match that of winning the Championship, the day will live with me forever. It was the best single day of cricket I have ever played in.

I doubt whether anyone connected with the club will ever forget the atmosphere. Lord's was packed, naturally, but the staggering thing was that 80 per cent of the crowd, maybe even more, came from Essex. The noise was unbelievable as Mike Denness and Graham Gooch walked out to open the batting for us against Surrey, and the level of support never faltered throughout the day.

We had beaten Yorkshire in the semi-final, which was virtually a cup final come early for me, and the county suddenly seemed obsessed by Cup fever, rather as Liverpool or Manchester is taken over by the grip of soccer if one of their teams reaches Wembley. For us, however, it was something entirely new, and there were nerves and superstitions to deal with, quite apart from the problems of beating a rejuvenated Surrey side.

I must admit I was nervous that day. After more than fifty Tests, I had butterflies squirming around my stomach when I tossed up on a glorious sunny morning – but I also had the feeling that this, at last, was going to be our day. And so it proved. Goochie made a classic 100, Kenny McEwan added 72 and we reached 290 for 6 in 55 overs. Surely it was beyond Surrey? But complacency never entered any of our heads, and it was just as well, for Surrey made a magnificent fight of it and only went down by 35 runs.

The moment of victory was magical. I remember leaping in the air, throwing my arms around J. K. Lever, who had appropriately taken the last wicket, and then being carried away in the celebration feeling. Even taking all my England experiences into account, it was the greatest day of my career.

9

Taking Charge of England

Mike Brearley had been restored to the England captaincy in June of 1981, with astonishing results. English cricket was depressed, following two defeats against the West Indies and a poor start to the Ashes series at home. Ian Botham resigned, and by a glorious coincidence recaptured his most outrageous form under Brearley's astute leadership. The result was a revival which will never be forgotten by any who witnessed it: victories at Leeds, Birmingham and Manchester, and the Ashes retained.

For the selectors, however, it was a brief respite from the problem of finding a long-term leader. They seemed no nearer a solution, but with Brearley unavailable for the winter tour of India, they had to try something new. . . .

Alec Bedser likes to be on the golf course early at weekends, which probably explains why my telephone rang at 7.45 a.m. on the morning of Saturday 29 August. To be honest, I would not have minded answering that call at 3.45 a.m., because it brought the news I had not dared to expect, the news I wanted more than anything else in life at that time.

In the time it took dear old Alec to go through the formalities of asking if I would accept the job, and me to do the right thing and say how I would be delighted to, a thousand thoughts ran through my mind. Uppermost among them, however, was the nagging fear that the trip to India might very easily be aborted for reasons which had precious little connection with cricket.

I have never accepted the involvement of politics in sport. Say I am naïve if you like, but I believe sportsmen should be able to play with and against anyone they choose. It should be above interference, and while I agree it is not always easy to implement such a policy, how much friendlier the world might be if every nation could get together on sports fields without their governments bickering about it.

In our case, the sensitive area was South Africa. It usually is in cricket. Geoff Boycott had been put on the so-called blacklist by the United Nations following his latest visit to the country, and there were rumours that the Indians would refuse to accept him as one of our party. We did not know it at the time, but Geoff Cook – who had captained Eastern Province in the South African Currie Cup – fell into the same category.

For some weeks before my appointment the newspapers had been carrying stories throwing doubts on the future of the tour. Many were based purely on rumour, and it certainly seemed that no one in authority in the Indian government had yet spoken decisively on the issue. But an issue it certainly was. I knew there was a good chance that I could join the 'élite' group of men who have been made captain of a tour which never takes place.

I tried not to dwell on it. After all, the England captaincy is not offered every day, so why waste the moment with gloomy speculation? For a couple of days, I could not keep the smile off my face. It was a marvellous feeling. Not a complete surprise, of course, because my name had been mentioned among the runners for the job in the press for some while. The waiting had been the difficult part, knowing I was the favourite to succeed Mike Brearley but not wanting to anticipate anything and then find myself let down. I had been overlooked before by England. I knew how it could hurt.

My first job was to tell Sue. Not that I needed to. She knew by the grin on my face as I replaced the receiver. We enjoyed breakfast that day. Then I had to talk to the Essex team. I decided to let them know what the position was that same day, even though the announcement was not being made until the following morning. We had a vital John Player League match on the Sunday, and I did not want them involved in the pressure and paraphernalia which comes inevitably with such an appointment.

As it turned out, I should probably have known better. The lads, notably East and Pont of course, did nothing but take the mickey all weekend, even standing back and making me walk half-way to the middle alone, self-conscious about the applause of the crowd as the public address system crackled the news. Typical.

Choosing the team for the tour contained its share of surprises for me. Like everyone else, I arrived at the meeting with my own idea of how the party should be made up.

The press and public seized on the fact that we only picked two spinners. India has a reputation, undeserved these days, for being a spinners' paradise, but we felt – unanimously here – that a third spinner would end up kicking his heels. I was happy with that selection. What we did wrong later was play only one spinner instead of both in most of the Tests. But that is another story.

There was a little more than two months between my being named captain, and stepping on the plane which took us to Bombay. But only a little more than two days in which I really believed we would be going.

The weeks which followed the end of the English season were depressing. India's objection to Boycott and Cook was confirmed by the government. They said they would not allow them to play. We said we would not come without them. It was a desperate stalemate, or so it seemed to me, and as Sue and I set off for a short holiday in Scotland late in October, I had reconciled myself to the abandonment of the tour.

We were driving home from that holiday when the news on Radio Two stated categorically that the tour was off. I was not surprised, but dreadfully disappointed, and as I drove in a gloomy sort of silence – Sue glancing sideways at me and knowing all too well what I was thinking – I considered the options open to the Test and County Cricket Board.

The least likely alternative was to have no tour at all. Even at that stage, it seemed certain that a free winter would encourage a full-scale exodus of England players to South Africa for just the sort of unofficial tour that the authorities had been battling to resist. So we would probably go instead to New Zealand. They had already confirmed their willingness to host a short tour, and it would be preferable to nothing at all. But I knew, in my heart, that nothing could replace the Indian trip to which I had been looking forward so much.

When I reached home the radio and a phone call or two brought renewed hope. The news bulletin I had heard in the car was inaccurate. No decision had been taken. The waiting had to go on. Finally, we were within seventy-two hours of departure when agreement was reached. Boycott and Cook were allowed to come, having both expressed their opposition to apartheid. Nothing could stop us now.

It was five years since my last England tour, but I knew too well that the last couple of weeks before departure could be unpleasant. The family know you will be away for a matter of months, and however hard you may try to cram in as much time with them as possible, there is no escape from the strain which mixes with the excitement of the challenge ahead. This time, though, there was no chance to think too much about it. I hardly had time to complete my packing before I was aboard the plane and away.

It may sound immodest, but I found it relatively simple to adjust to captaining England. I had, after all, been skippering Essex for eight years, so the basics of the job were hardly new to me. I happen to like India, which was a large bonus. Dealing with the press has never intimidated me, so that part of my responsibility did not weigh heavily, as I know it has on some.

By the end of the tour, despite our 1–0 defeat, I had no hesitation in saying that we were still the better side. Equally, India proved that they are far more capable than many people gave them credit for. Kapil Dev makes a huge difference to them, as he would to any Test side in the world. For the first time in their international history, India have a potent strike bowler to complement their

91

traditional spinning strength – and Kapil can bat a bit, too! The class of Gavaskar and Viswanath remained obvious, even late in their respective careers, and I left India with a very good impression of the tall and serious-looking all-rounder, Ravi Shastri.

I also came home with the distinct feeling that India would be easier to beat on English soil. I was looking forward to proving the point. But, as everyone now knows, it was not to be.

The age-old myths about Indian sanitation, prevalent diseases and essential diets are now largely redundant. Certain of the up-country venues are still not the type of places where one would choose to spend a holiday, but the cities, in which we spent most of our time, are now lively, cosmopolitan centres with hotels to rival the best in the world. Those who had not been before naturally feared the worst, and stocked up with pills to protect against all kinds of stomach illnesses, but in fact we escaped very lightly in that respect. Instead, most of us suffered chills and viruses which had very little to do with Indian food, and everything to do with the itinerary we were asked to undertake.

Contrary to popular opinion, not everywhere in India is hot. Some places, indeed, are positively cold, while others can scorch like an open oven. For pasty-faced Englishmen, arriving out of a British winter, a period of acclimatization is essential, and too much switching from hot to cold clearly undesirable. It sounds like simple common sense, but the logic apparently escaped the notice of the people who drew up our itinerary.

Ideally, the first Test should be staged in Delhi, the northernmost venue and the coolest of all the Test centres. We began there in 1976–7, when I played under Tony Greig, and then moved slowly southwards during the series, with the final Test in the baking atmosphere of Bombay.

But not this time. We had to start at Bombay, where the sun peels and swells the skin, and then make haphazard strides up and down the country, hot to cold, cold to hot, which resulted in the most absurd fortnight imaginable. The reason the Indians offered was the world hockey event in Bombay – no comfort to us.

We began those two weeks in the pleasant heat of Madras, at a dry 85 degrees – a very agreeable climate. From there we went to Indore, which was cold, on to Cuttack and a one-day international in intense heat, and so to Kanpur for a Test played throughout in chilly, bleak weather like April at Derby. Just to complete the joke, we then had to find our way by means of several aircraft changes to Colombo for a spell in the world's hottest cricket country, Sri Lanka.

Inside that fortnight, we had travelled 4000 miles and endured four extreme changes of temperature. No wonder very few of us escaped without catching colds and 'flu. Through it all, our team spirit remained superb. In the bad, bleak times, like the rare country games when we were jousting with rats in our rooms and toying with soggy omelettes as the only tolerable food, there was always a joker in the pack to make us laugh about the situation.

It was the same when things went wrong on the field. Just as well, too, because we needed that spirit very early in the tour. At Bombay, we lost a Test which was ultimately to decide the series, and I am sorry to say I reckon we lost it because we were undermined by the worst umpiring I have ever encountered.

Let me be plain. I hate moaning about umpires, more particularly after a defeat. Whatever the motives, whatever the provocation, it smacks of sour grapes, and I have no doubt we were widely accused of showing just such bad sportsmanship after Bombay. But this was more than just the occasional incompetent decision. One umpire in particular was dreadful. All kinds of words floated agonizingly through my head during and after that match, but because I was captain of England I had to remain silent. That was frustration personified.

It is wrong to call any umpire a cheat, because bias can never satisfactorily be proved. Suffice it to say our full report on this umpire, lodged in the usual manner at the end of the game, included a recommendation that he should never stand again for a first-class game.

Imagine our feelings, therefore, when we discovered his appointment to umpire our one-day international at Cuttack, towards the end of the trip. We found out by accident, in transit to Cuttack at Bangalore airport. There, in the same lounge, was the man the press had nicknamed 'The Butcher of Bombay'. Incredulous, I asked him what he was doing there. Silly question, really, because I already knew the answer, and he had to confirm it.

It was the first time in my cricket career that I had been obliged to handle a full-scale controversy over umpires, and handle it from a position of involvement as well as a position of responsibility, as I was one of those who felt strongly that my own dismissal was unfair, during the first innings of our demise at Bombay.

We had negotiated a good position, at 95 for 1 in reply to India's 179, and nothing short of 300 figured in our ambitions. But in an afternoon session on the second day that I will never forget, our middle-order was wiped out by the umpire. David Gower was adjudged run out when he was virtually becalmed in his crease with his bat grounded, Ian Botham was 'caught' at slip off his elbow and John Emburey and myself were victims of strange thinking on the l.b.w. law.

Nine wickets went down for 71 runs and when the Indians set us to score 241 to win, we never looked like making a fist of it. Allegations that we batted with a complex about the umpiring are probably true and certainly regrettable. But although we talked until most of us were blue in the face, trying hard to convince ourselves that the game was still there to be won, it is impossible to forget about the threat of the finger while you are actually out there. What made it more difficult was the fact that the umpire seemed to steadfastly object to raising his finger when India were batting.

In the course of the match Sunil Gavaskar made 69 runs and batted better than almost anyone. But we all believed he was out twice, in each innings, before we finally won our case. We dismissed India twice, and genuinely believed that we had actually taken 16 wickets in each innings.

Our players became depressed, understandably so, because confidence drains from even the best in such a situation. And if our friend was the worst umpire we met, by some distance, there were plenty of others who fell short of the standards we have come to expect in England.

Part of the captain's duty is to concentrate the minds of his men on the job in hand, forcing them to forget about outside pressures – and that must include umpires. But in this instance, I am not sure I succeeded. At least, if I did, it took a very long time.

Our bowlers began to question the umpires, asking them why they had given an l.b.w. not out. It probably did nothing but antagonize them further, but the point was reached when that did not seem to matter. We knew we would get nothing from them anyway.

Graham Gooch sank to the lowest ebb of all the batsmen, probably because he suffered from more poor decisions than anyone else. The tide was to turn for him later in the trip, but when things were at their worst and he did not seem able to get past 20 without being shot out, he said to me that he might as well go home, for all the good he was doing trying to bat against such odds. Thankfully, he did not pursue the idea.

I took out my frustrations on a bail at Bangalore, and found myself obliged to write letters of apology and attend specially convened press conferences to explain my apparent petulance.

The circumstances were these. Second Test, first innings. Our objective was to bat for two days, score 400 and attempt to bowl out the Indians twice. It was a tall order, and we had our moments of trouble; I was at the crease at the end of the first day and still there the next morning. I saw off the new ball, survived a difficult period against Kapil Dev . . . and was then given out caught behind off a ball from Shastri which I could not claim to have got my bat anywhere near.

At that moment I suppose the red mists were upon me.

I had been in India for about six weeks, and felt happy with only one of the seven dismissals I had suffered. It sounds absurd, I know, but it was true. And the frustrations had built up to such a point that far worse things were going through my mind than the tap of a bail with my bat which I finally administered on my way off. I felt like flattening all three stumps.

I know it was wrong. An apology was called for, and I gave it unreservedly, writing to Mr Wankhede, the President of the Indian Board. It was something I have never done before on a pitch, and I sincerely hope I never do it again. But, looked at clinically, it illustrates to perfection the feelings that were raging inside us all at that time in the tour.

Probably the batsman who profited most from the umpiring was Sunil Gavaskar. We apparently had to accept that it would be a crime to get him out in India. Like all the other lads, I grew increasingly ratty when he survived time after time against appeals of great confidence, but we could not hold it against him personally. Ian Botham and I went to dinner at Sunil's house one night and, typical Botham, he quickly brought up the subject of the umpiring. It did not spoil the evening, though, and I must say I came to like Gavaskar as a person as the tour went on. A great batsman and good company – but if he had one tendency bound to annoy it was his inclination to slow down events to an almost farcical degree.

Slow play, and blatant time-wasting, were among the most contentious issues of the tour. I did not escape the criticism, and many people apparently thought we should have been making more positive attempts to speed things up when we were in the field. But that is all too easy to say from a distance of several thousand miles – very much more difficult out in the middle at Bangalore, or Calcutta.

The first consideration is that most of the pitches were loaded in favour of the batsmen. Last time we toured there, in 1976, India had four world-class spin bowlers so, not surprisingly, the wickets were tailored to their advantage. This time we were at least equally strong in that department and we knew there would be very little

So often, Essex had been edged into the runners-up position
in the John Player League. But in 1981 they won it by a
clear six points

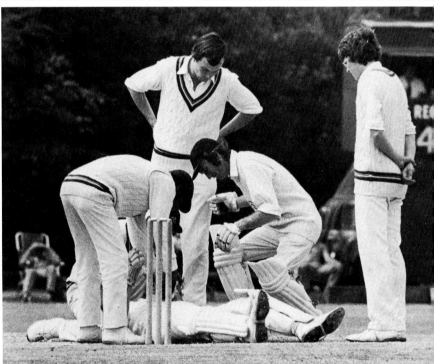

Top: Sometimes you are on top of the world at the end of an innings – but occasionally things can seem very bleak!

Bottom: The caring captain. Fletcher tends to team-mate Stuart Turner, pole-axed by a Mike Procter bouncer

Indian memories . . . swooping for a short-leg catch (top
left), square-cutting Dilip Doshi (top right) and looking back
in horror (bottom)

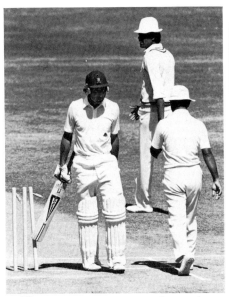

The moment a temper was lost and a storm broke in Bangalore

Taking refreshment with Graham Gooch, England's greatest loss to the South African conflict

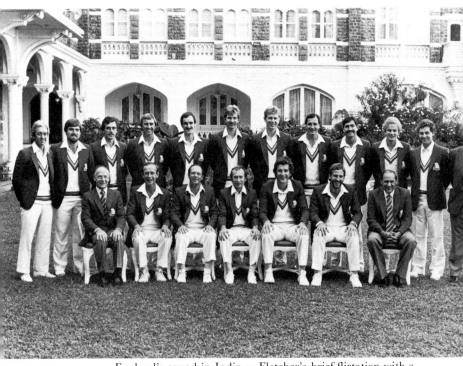

England's squad in India — Fletcher's brief flirtation with a dream

A high moment on tour — sharing champagne with a great
friend, John Lever

A low moment at home — Fletcher sits under the Oval
scoreboard, a spectator at a one-day international after his
sacking

The ultimate escape — away from it all for a day with only
the gun and the countryside for company

turn in the pitches; no more than the naturally dusty conditions enforced, anyway. The pitch at Bombay for the first Test was always likely to provide a result, and we happened to be on the wrong end of it, so from that moment on we were predictably condemned to some of the slowest, flattest pitches any of us had seen.

At least three of the remaining five pitches were too good for any kind of contest. If you wanted to bat for two days, unconcerned about the pace of scoring, it is impossible to imagine better conditions.

But this was only part of our problem. Equally damaging to any chance we had of winning a Test was the erosion of the time available by a number of regular factors. One concerned the balls, which went out of shape twice a session, without fail. This might not have been so bad but for the fact that the umpires never carried a selection of alternative balls of various ages. Instead, a new ball was produced each time, and a pantomime began which at first seemed highly amusing but became more irritating with each new day. The umpires used sandpaper to scrape the shine off the ball, then rubbed it in the dust to simulate further wear. The whole operation would probably take five minutes which, when it is occurring several times each day, thieves a chunk out of the 5½ hours' playing time.

Likewise, the drinks intervals. Now I would be the first to concede that there are times in India when a mid-session drink is a necessity rather than a preference. But there are others when the weather is cooler than in England and the operation is superfluous. We often asked to forego the drinks intervals if we were in the field, but it made no difference. The batsmen, and the umpires come to that, insisted on refreshment, and so the circus wagon – a brightly coloured trolley and a cast of a thousand waiters, it often seemed – was pushed on yet again, and another five minutes slipped by while we seethed silently in the middle.

Time-wasting was the third factor. The Indians might flinch at the expression, because they seemed to see nothing sinister in the lack of activity. But to us, accustomed to hurrying through our overs with the threat of fines hanging over us, it was sheer purgatory.

Even the Indian spinners managed to drag out an over for almost four minutes, pausing between each delivery to make minute field changes, then wandering back to their mark-up as if in slow motion. Often, Gavaskar would halt a bowler as he was about to run up, and walk with deliberation from slip for a conference, the content of which was seldom clear.

Batsmen were not beyond a ploy or two, either. I have never seen so much 'gardening' done on impeccable pitches, nor more mid-wicket conversations, nor more lengthy and studious contemplations of field setting. It became something of a joke, a sick one for us.

It has been said that we joined in and slowed the game down just as much as the Indians. I cannot entirely refute that, because the evidence is that we didn't bowl our overs any quicker. But the Indians were getting through 11 overs an hour with two spinners bowling, whereas we invariably had at least one seamer. If we had tried, and not too hard at that, we could have bowled 6 overs an hour and – here is the significant part – not received a word of reprimand from the umpires or a moment's barracking from the crowd.

Umpires in England would have put a stop to such tactics very early in the series, but the Indians did nothing and said nothing. If it had happened in this country to such an extent – and I estimate we often lost an hour's play a day through all these things – the spectators would have walked out in disgust and a justifiable fuss would have been made by the press. In India the crowds appeared not to notice and the newspapers dismissed the issue.

More overs are bowled in three-day Championship games in England than in five-day Tests during that series, and there was very little we could do about it. Only after playing there personally can you appreciate the problems of trying to be positive – something stifles you at every turn.

Boredom became the worst of everyone's problems. In

more than one Test, we knew with some confidence by lunchtime on the first day that there was no chance of a result. Our only hope generally lay in trying to make 450-plus, then aiming to bowl the Indians out twice. But there was never enough time. We came close once or twice – but not very close.

Several players came home disillusioned with Test cricket. There had been no problems in discipline and team spirit had remained remarkably high. But by the end, I could sense most of them had taken enough of the frustrations and wanted nothing more than to go home.

Before they could do that, we had to go to Sri Lanka for another Test, the first ever on the island. If there was a lack of enthusiasm in advance, the place itself cheered us all up. We were wonderfully looked after and, what is more, the Test turned out to be a good one. Sri Lanka proved to be a good side in their own conditions, and after three days' play they held a good chance of beating us. Then they froze. In the last two days they discovered a great deal about the pressures of Test cricket and John Emburey preyed on their nerves and bowled us to victory.

Emburey had been affected more than most by the Indian experience. He and Graham Gooch spent a great deal of time together, and I knew that they had both been soured against touring, and against Test cricket abroad. They could see no point in playing when the game had such a negative bias.

I could see that some sympathetic talking, and firm encouragement, might be needed in both their cases before the home Test season began. But as things turned out, it was not necessary. Emburey and Gooch were banned, and I was dropped.

Two topics dominated cricket conversation in the early months of 1982, and Geoff Boycott was concerned prominently in both. First, he returned home from the Indian tour in early January, suffering from illness. Then, only days after the rest of the party returned, it was Boycott who led out a clandestine group of players to South Africa for a tour which was to have grave and controversial consequences, including the suspension from Test cricket for three years of all those involved – and they included Gooch and Emburey.

My career and Geoffrey Boycott's had begun around the same time. We were both capped by our county in 1963, and in subsequent years we played together for England, and in opposition at county level, on countless occasions. Twice before, we had toured together and I knew all about Boycott's idiosyncrasies, his reclusive nature and what often seemed awkward unsociability. The last time had been in the West Indies on the 1973–4 tour under Mike Denness, and he had not been easy there, partly because he imagined he should have been leading the team himself. But the rest of the players tended to ignore him, let him live his individual existence and be thankful for his runs. In India this time there was no such tolerance.

As captain, I had naturally been pleased to have him in the party, because he remained one of the finest openers in the world. But when the tour began, I was prepared for the possibility that he might need careful treatment; in meetings with the manager, Raman Subba Row, and my vice-captain, Bob Willis, I had discussed with them the best way of handling Boycott to everyone's satisfaction. It may sound absurd, having to devote such thought to one player, but Boycott is no ordinary character and a captain's duty is to work out every personality in his squad and decide on a policy towards him.

On the early stages of the trip Boycott was no different from how I remembered him. Off the field, one seldom saw him. He would turn up at team meetings, but never had a drink with the lads, and rarely ate in company with us. Fair enough – no one should decry him for that. In cricket affairs we got on pretty well. I valued his advice on tactical matters and sought it frequently. He sometimes needed pushing before giving his opinions, but there is no doubt his views are sound, particularly on pitches.

Geoff was batting well, and when he broke Gary Sobers's record number of Test runs, during the Delhi Test on 23 December, it must have been one of the most richly satisfying moments of his career. I felt genuinely delighted for him, because I knew it meant a lot, and I was also very aware what a benefit his runs had been to England over the years. But already, behind the scenes, things were happening which contributed to his early homeward flight.

On every tour there are certain social commitments on players which are accepted as being compulsory. In all the Test centres of India, and most of the country venues too, at least one official function had been arranged for us. We were expected to attend, wearing blazers and tour ties, and generally mix with the local dignitaries for an hour or two.

There are always some people in the squad who find these affairs difficult, and it has to be said that there are times when it is hard to treat them as more than a chore. But we are ambassadors for our country, as well as Test cricketers, when on tour, and we are paid well enough these days to put up with occasional inconvenience.

Boycott did not appear to think that included him. At many receptions he sat down in a corner and seemed thoroughly unco-operative. He became an embarrassment. His relations with Raman were strained by his habit of calling him 'The Diplomat', and saying it in a sneering fashion which made it quite plain it was more than a piece of fun.

Boycott did his job on the field. His responsibility, as always, was to give our innings a solid start, and more often than not he succeeded. But in Delhi, just after he had broken Sobers's record, a baffling saga of ill-feeling developed over my comments to the press about slow scoring. I had made the mistake of saying that I had already spoken to Chris Tavare and Boycott on the matter; in fact, I had not at that stage had the opportunity of discussing it with Boycott, but knew I would be doing so long before the journalists' stories appeared in print.

The next day, however, Boycott's lady friend Anne Wyatt arrived in India bearing copies of every morning newspaper, and before long I found myself confronted by an angry man brandishing various articles with sections underlined. Boycott had scoured every paper and picked out sections with which he disagreed. Although by then I had talked over our scoring rate with him, he was annoyed that I had mentioned it to the press first, and demanded an apology.

Raman and I spent hours on the subject, much of the time poring over the newspaper pieces and trying to assess just what it was Boycott objected to. We never did work that out. It seemed an insignificant matter to make such a fuss about, and I could not imagine any other player doing it. To maintain any sort of harmony, however, the thing had to be smoothed over, and although I felt he did not deserve an apology, it seemed the simplest way out.

It was only a few days after he had achieved his personal aims and become the highest run-maker of all time, that Boycott fell ill. He saw a High Commission doctor in Delhi, then retired to his bed in Calcutta, claiming that the sudden drop in temperatures in Jammu – which rests in the foothills of the Himalayas – had given him a chill. Nobody would deny that possibility, for I have already mentioned the wild variance in temperatures during our itinerary. Boycott had been given the next match off, but rather than join the other free players for four days at Fishermen's Cove, near Madras, he wanted to go back to see his doctor in Delhi. We felt, however, that the team should not be split any more than necessary, and if he needed to recuperate, Fishermen's Cove was an ideal place to do so. This did not go down well with Boycott.

He had batted well in the first innings of the Calcutta Test, but did not field. This was the game when we came closest to an equalizing win; there is reason to suggest that if the weather had been kinder on the last morning, when a thick smog blanketed the ground and held up play, we might even have pulled it back. But by lunchtime we had to accept that we had been thwarted again.

We returned to the dressing-room deflated and I, for

one, was scarcely able to believe the news we were greeted with. Boycott had apparently turned up at the ground during the morning, ostensibly to pack his bag for the onward journey. But while there, he had said that he intended playing golf for the rest of the day, and asked if any of the other players not in the team would care to join him.

I am pleased to relate they all refused – but not half as pleased as I was to hear it from their own mouths. One player going absent without leave was bad enough; two or three would have been a disaster.

Of course, we did not take it for granted that Geoff had gone to the golf course. We had to check, because it seemed such an amazing thing to do. Here we were, desperately trying to win a Test match in the most arduous of conditions, and a man whose place, had he been fit, was on the field with us apparently decides he might have a gentle round of golf. It made no sense, but it made me very angry.

We telephoned the secretary of the golf club, whom we had come to know over the past week or so. The golf club was quite a haven from the hustle and bustle of Calcutta life, and most of us had been there on free days, either to play or simply relax. The secretary confirmed the story. Yes, Geoff was there. Yes, he had been playing since before lunch.

That evening we called a meeting of the tour management committee and, after some general discussion on the matter, we telephoned Boycott in his room and asked him to join us. It was at least twenty minutes before he arrived. I told him precisely what I thought of his behaviour that day and passed on the reactions of the team. It apparently came as no surprise to him; indeed, he had arrived prepared for it. If that was how everyone felt, he said, then he thought he should resign from the tour party. With that, he handed us a pre-written note to that effect.

It was almost unheard of for an England player to quit midway through a tour, and in such controversial circumstances, but we were prepared to accept it. Boycott agreed that an apology to the remainder of the team was in order, and wrote it out on the spot.

Having slept on the problem, the committee reconvened at 7.30 the following morning, and agreed that Boycott's resignation should be accepted and arrangements made for him to fly home. Raman and I went to his room to tell him. To our surprise, he had changed his mind. Now, he said, he did not want to go home after all. He knew he had done wrong and he had been happy to apologize, but he wanted to go on playing for England. He was plainly cut up about it, so we agreed to go back once again and consult with the other members of the committee.

Now we were faced with a decision. Geoff suddenly wanted to stay, so if it were agreed that he should return to England, we were effectively sending him home. We discussed the matter once more and concluded that he was clearly in no state to consider playing Test cricket. We decided it would be better for him, and for us, if he went home.

The next problem was communicating this information to the rest of the squad, who had already flown out of Calcutta heading for Jamshedpur, an up-country steel town and venue for a three-day game against East Zone. Bernard Thomas was in charge of the side, and we told him by telephone. He broke the news at breakfast time on the first morning of the match, so by the time I arrived at nine o'clock, everyone was up to date.

I had not expected tearful recriminations, but the relief with which the news appeared to have been greeted still surprised me.

Boycott's apparent reluctance to contribute anything to a tour off the field had made it very clear to me that he should never tour with England again. Possibly, he could have played again in a home series, although if the same players were still in the England side, I would not have envied him his reception.

Strangely, however, he was touring again within a few

days of the England trip ending – and with several of the men he had so angered only weeks earlier. It was, of course, an unofficial tour. So unofficial, so secret, that most of those taking part were not certain of their own involvement until twenty-four, or maybe forty-eight hours before flying out of Heathrow for South Africa. Not that the tour had been thrown together in a hurry. Indeed, in a sense it had been planned for years. Many times such visits had been mooted, players had been sounded out, provisional itineraries even drawn up. But apart from one or two unrepresentative multi-national sides, nothing had ever come to fruition. This was different.

For more than a year there had been mounting speculation about an England side going there. Invitations had been put about during the tour to the West Indies, early in 1981, I understand, and it was Boycott who acted as the middle-man and sounded out his fellow players.

During the summer which followed, there were attempts to put together at least two separate tours, but neither succeeded. Only when we reached India, I now know, did things start to happen again.

Silly as it may sound, I was kept in the dark throughout the tour. My only hint that anything might be in the wind came in a question from Boycott. We were together somewhere on a rest day and he casually asked me if I would be prepared to play cricket in South Africa. Nothing more, nothing less. I thought briefly, though not too deeply, and replied that in my current position as England captain I would not. I honestly heard nothing more about the proposed venture until we were back in England.

While we were in Sri Lanka the English press carried a story that Ian Botham might be going to South Africa. I tackled him, and he said that he had turned down an approach two months earlier. Still I knew nothing.

There were plenty of rumours flying around in the couple of days after we arrived home, but the first confirmation I received came in a call from Donald Carr, Secretary of the Test and County Cricket Board. He said he was phoning to ask if I was one of those going to South

Africa as part of an England XI. I was able to tell him, in all honesty, that I knew nothing about it. I still don't know if he believed me!

His call came on the Friday, two days after our return. The players flew out on Saturday and Sunday, and on the Sunday night my telephone at home was ringing again; international, this time, but with a familiar voice at the other end. It was Goochie, ringing from Johannesburg and in a businesslike mood. He said he had somebody with him who wanted to talk to me, and then passed the phone to a man named Locke, one of the organizers of the venture. Mr Locke explained that it had been felt I should not be approached while captaining England on tour; now it was my turn to wonder if I should believe my ears. He added, however, that they were keen that I should captain the English side and went on to outline the schedule. If I were in South Africa by the following Thursday, 4 March, he could guarantee I would be home again by 1 April. He offered me £45,000 for the four weeks.

The temptation to snatch at such money was one side of it. The feeling of having achieved an ambition and won the England captaincy, something I wanted to keep, was another. It was not a decision I could make in a matter of seconds on the phone, so I asked for time. Mr Locke allowed me twenty-four hours.

I talked it over with two people. One was Sue, of course, and the other was Clem Driver, the Essex scorer, my benefit chairman and a man whose opinions I have always respected. Clem promised to phone me back later that evening, and by the time he did, around 11 p.m., Sue and I had made up our minds that I should turn down the offer. Clem had independently come to the same conclusion.

The next morning I phoned Doug Insole, a leading figure at Essex and in the TCCB. I told him of the offer and of my decision. His relief was audible, even down a phone line.

There was time to think then. I considered the men

106

who had gone, several of them very close friends and two – Gooch and John Lever – team-mates at Essex. That John had gone, I could easily understand. He knew very well that his England days were numbered; he had probably made his last tour, so why shouldn't he cash in on the vast sums being offered? I did not think anyone in their right mind could blame him for going, just as no one should blame the likes of Dennis Amiss – maybe even Boycott.

Goochie disappointed me. I knew he was a little fed up with the length and the strains of England tours, and I could imagine that his deal with the South Africans must cover more than a single year and be worth a vast amount of money. But I could not help returning to the fact that he had another five or six years at his peak. What an asset he could have been to the England side in that time.

Even my thoughts, you notice, were in the past tense when it came to Test cricket, for it seemed very obvious that a ban would have to be implemented. Despite some hysterical calls for a full-scale suspension from county cricket as well, there was no reason to suspect that might happen. Restraint of trade was a term to make the cricket authorities wince since the expensive High Court case over Kerry Packer, and legal advice would be sought and confirmed before any action was taken. But surely, no one who committed himself to a South African tour did so with his eyes closed?

In principle, I was not against the trip. For some years I had felt that the policy of isolation against South Africa was self-defeating, and that far more good could be achieved by playing against them and encouraging the right sort of change.

I am no supporter of apartheid, but nor do I think it is confined to South Africa. In different forms it exists in most places where cricket is played. I find the caste system in India equally abhorrent, and certain parts of the West Indies exercise a discrimination against the white man – no one says very much about that. Always, it seems to be South Africa which suffers. Our athletes and soccer

107

players can compete against Russia without a murmur of protest; three British football teams even went to the World Cup in 1982, to play alongside and possibly against Argentina while we were still technically at war with them. The inconsistencies are baffling and hypocritical.

10

Winter Work and Worries

*One of the popular misconceptions about cricketers is that they are
paid enough money during the summer to permit them a lazy
winter. It just is not true, and dozens of first-class players in
England have a perennial battle to find off-season employment.
For the lucky, talented few, the problem is removed by touring with
England, for which all players are paid a fee – recently dramatically increased. Keith made six overseas trips in nine winters
between 1968, the year he married Sue, and 1977, but the interim
times still caused some anxieties.*

Someone threatened to kill me during the late winter
months of 1970. I don't know who the man was and,
thankfully, I have never set eyes on him since, but the
threat was couched in strong enough terms for the police
to take an interest.

Ironically, it had nothing whatever to do with cricket,
except for the fact that a newspaper had decided to run
a picture-story on me under the heading 'Where do cricketers go in the winter?' This time it was the *Daily Sketch*
but the idea is a hardy annual for popular papers with a
few column inches to fill during the bad weather, and it
often throws up an interesting subject or two.

It was well known within the game that I was keen on
shooting, so when the *Sketch* reporter contacted me, he
asked if they could photograph me out in the fields with
a gun under one arm and a brace of pheasants in my
hand. He asked me a few questions and I explained that
I was actually involved in gamekeeping work on a vol-
untary basis that winter. My introduction to this had

come from my good friend Danny Northrop, who ran a shoot in the nearby village of Barrington and had 2000 acres and 500 pheasants to protect. There were six shoots during the season, which runs from October to January, and Danny had asked me to help him around the estate in my spare time. There was no overseas tour that winter so I had eagerly accepted. I did about as much work as I wanted around the farms and thoroughly enjoyed it all.

Most of it came very naturally to a bloke who had grown up in this very rural part of England. I had always considered shooting as English a sport as cricket and I had first handled a gun at about the same age I first used a cricket bat.

It was not a regular job; much more something I did to help Danny when I visited him. It gave me exercise and kept me outdoors, so it was beneficial, too. Feeding the pheasants was one of the main duties, of course, but we also had to set traps for the vermin which would harm them, such as rats, stoats and weasels, and check them regularly.

I carried a shotgun whenever I was on the estate, but seldom used it. When I was not feeding or trapping I was on patrol for poachers. Plenty of suspicious-looking characters would hang around the fringes of the property, but the sight of me with a gun was usually enough to scare them off.

On the organized days I took part in shooting for pheasant and partridge and found that I had to adapt my style with a gun. As a lad, I used to come up behind the birds and shoot them as they were flying away from me. But in formal shoots the birds are driven towards the guns, which at first I found difficult to cope with.

At no time did I think of it as a cruel sport, but rather a part of British heritage. Just occasionally, a bird would escape, wounded, after being hit, and perhaps be picked up by a fox. That, to me, is one of the ways of nature.

All of this came out in the *Sketch*'s feature, together with a vivid picture of myself in hat, anorak and wellingtons, plus gun and birds. It was only a matter of days later that I received a letter, abusing me for subscribing to such a cruel pastime and threatening to shoot me when next I walked outside the door of my home. Fortunately, my nature is not prone to panic over such things. I laughed it off, dismissed the writer as an obvious crank, and would have thought no more about it but for the effect it clearly had on Sue. We were in only the second year of our marriage and she was not keen to see me finished off quite so dramatically, so she insisted on passing the letter to the police.

They went through the motions of coming to interview me, and asked if I had ever received threatening letters before. I told them that every time I missed a catch or got out for 0, someone was angry enough to write and call me names, if not exactly endanger my life. I have had an assortment of letters from cranks every year since I started playing and I have no reason to suspect they will stop. But this, the police insisted, was different, and they warned me to take various precautions while they investigated the matter. I am pretty sure they never discovered the identity of the writer, though.

That was the most serious, but by no means the only letter I received on the subject from anti-blood-sports types. That article seemed to have given them a target for their feelings, but I did not hold it against any of them, apart from those who became hysterically abusive.

It happened occasionally in pubs, too. I would be having a quiet drink with Sue, or with a couple of pals, and suddenly I would find myself being spoken to in rude and aggressive tones by someone who had recognized me and knew of my hobby. Usually, anyone setting up an argument in such a public place had been drinking heavily, and I had nothing to gain by getting involved. My usual reaction was to tell the bloke he was entitled to his opinion and then ignore him. If he persisted, I would leave the pub and go somewhere else.

I still shoot nowadays, each winter I am at home. Nothing has happened to put me off the sport and I enjoy it tremendously. I now have no time to help out my gamekeeping friend as I have a regular winter job, but I still clearly remember the years when close-seasons without a tour provided me with major problems.

In the autumn of 1969 I did what I thought was natural and signed on the dole. I had been married six months and could not afford a winter without income. To my astonishment, the Social Security rejected my claim, on the grounds that I was a seasonal earner and therefore never completely unemployed. Perhaps they expected me to meekly swallow their ruling; if so, they were badly mistaken. I spoke to my solicitor, who advised that I should take the matter to a tribunal. In court, he argued that I had come to expect that I would earn my living overseas during the close-season months. There was no England tour to support me that winter, however.

This was in many ways a test case for international cricketers and I won it convincingly. The chairman of the bench ruled that I was entitled to claim benefit for however many months I was idle between seasons or tours, and actually went so far as to tick off the clerk who allowed it to go as far as a tribunal. It appears that I had far better advice than the Social Security, who have not, to my knowledge, tried to prevent any other cricketers in that position from claiming dole money ever since.

There have been various stories of late about county cricketers joining the unemployment list because they are unable to gain winter work. This is obviously unfortunate; in an ideal world, no cricketer would have to scrape around to earn a living in the winter. To my mind, however, the blame for the situation must be divided: some clubs are badly run, missing out on opportunities to make use of their staff; and some players are just as lazy as certain other sections of the British working force.

I would make the general observation that county cricketers are underpaid, because their salary should be sufficient to see them through a year, not just through a season. The gulf between the Test and county player has become ridiculously wide in recent years. This was brought brutally home to me during 1982 when I suddenly reverted to being one of those average county players, having enjoyed all the benefits of the England captaincy for the previous few months.

I am not saying Test cricketers are overpaid. Their pay is about right when one considers they are at the very peak of what has become an increasingly commercial entertainment. But every county player is in the top 200 of his profession, and their rewards are a pittance compared, shall we say, to those of the top 200 singers, or even the top 200 doctors.

Even now, in this enlightened age of sponsorship, some counties do not sell themselves as well as they should, nor do they realize that their players have a very relevant role to play in the financial viability of the club.

The turnstiles are never going to click enough times to make any county club profitable, so those who are sensible and businesslike will look outside the game for the necessary backing. No county, for instance, should have to depend on the Test and County Cricket Board's pool of Test match profits to ensure it remains afloat. Any money from that source should principally be spent on ground improvements – and I say that in the knowledge that Essex devoted £70,000 of their TCCB share-out to developing the Chelmsford ground before the 1982 season. It is worth recording that Essex have 8000 members now; not so long ago, they barely topped the 3000 mark – and the difference is not, I am sure, entirely due to success on the field. It has emanated from hard work by everyone concerned.

I would maintain that the players have done a good deal to enhance the reputation of the club, and trace this back to Brian Taylor's period as captain. He may have been a traditionalist in some ways, an intimidating character in others, but he was quite shrewd enough to appreciate the value of players involving themselves in public relations activities. Very early in his spell in charge, he began encouraging all the players to accept invitations from clubs within the vicinity, particularly if this meant public speaking. Now many of us were not at all keen on this idea, myself included. I have already described how I froze, wordless, the first time I stood up to address a club gathering, and I am sure I was not the only one to suffer that humiliating fate. 'Tonker', however, could always see beyond a little bit of embarrassment and impressed upon us that a few evenings out of each of our lives, and just a little effort, could spread the word and deeds of the club to previously untapped corners of the county and, hopefully, attract a few new members each time. He was quite right. When I took over the captaincy I strove to perpetuate this policy and, as a result, most of our staff are now at least fundamentally experienced in public speaking. Some, like Ray East, are naturally in greater demand than others, but we try to spread the load among the players and, in general, it works pretty well. Within my own range of north Essex, I have discovered an enormous number of farmers who are keen on cricket and now regularly attend home Essex matches; even within my home village of Great Easton there is a substantial, loyal following.

Far be it from me to claim that all of Essex's viability is down to the players. Behind the scenes, largely inconspicuous but hugely industrious, we have a band of men who devote a great deal of their spare time to the club for virtually no tangible reward. Principal among them is Doug Insole, our vice-chairman, whose professional attitude and business acumen have taken the club into areas that previous generations would not have thought possible. A great number of companies are involved with the club now and our festival weeks – of which there are currently three – are all in profit before a ball is bowled, essential arithmetic in these days when to rely on gate-money is to invite disaster.

My point, however, is that the attraction of the players could be utilized – exploited, if you like – far more by the clubs than is the case at present. There can be no doubt that when a company takes a tent, or a box, for a day of a county game, the directors are eager that their customers should meet and chat with the likes of Graham Gooch. For many people who follow sport, but have no direct involvement, it will end a very sociable day in the perfect manner if they can rub shoulders with an international name. So we should not deny them that chance.

In my experience, players at Essex have only been asked to do this during a season, and then they have generally been very responsible about it. I am well aware that towards the end of a long, maybe unsuccessful season, some of the players would far rather slip away for a quiet drink by themselves than chat to sponsors' guests for half an hour, and there have been times when we have shown ourselves to be reluctant. But my own view has always been that it is part of our job to carry out these social duties and that cricketers in general do not do enough of them.

Counties could be encouraged to make better use of players in the close-season, perhaps engaging some on full-time contracts to travel around promoting the club – surely a cheap and effective way of raising membership and funds.

If clubs are short-sighted in this respect, however, players are not blameless. I know of many who have pleaded hardship during an off-season when, in truth, they have not lifted a finger to get a job. Their alternative may be a coaching appointment abroad, and it is true that some players are very reluctant to leave their families, but if such jobs are available I do not think any cricketer turning them down has the right to complain that no one will employ him.

I have been lucky, I admit that. Ten years ago I was approached by a man named Dick Burge, a keen cricket and soccer player who was working in an executive capacity for a leading oil company. He had been sent down to my part of Essex to implement the smooth takeover of a smaller company, and in gathering new staff he could see some value in having a well-known sporting figure on his sales side. Although I had no previous experience in that field, I agreed to give it a try, and it certainly seems to have been mutually successful as I still spend my winters working for Dick and have now built up something like 200 customers within a 40-mile radius of our Halstead office.

Certain newspapers printed a story that I was turning up to sell oil to farmers dressed in my MCC blazer so that they would be sure to recognize me. I can happily refute that in the knowledge that I would probably have pneumonia by now if I just wore a blazer and tie on some of my calls during the January freeze-ups. I doubt whether it would have won me any favours, anyway. I have found that most of the farmers on my route are interested in one sport or another, but they are certainly not the types to be impressed by a badge on a blazer!

The job arrived at a very good time. Tara, our elder daughter, was on the way. It was clear that I had to have something other than cricket to fall back on, if only as security for whenever I had to finish playing. At first I was apprehensive. Was this really the job for me? I wondered. Travelling around the county with the assignment of selling something I knew little about to people I did not know at all seemed a daunting prospect, and for a time it was certainly difficult. 'Cold selling' is never easy, and when the customer is a farmer who may be cursing the weather, or a hundred and one other things, a visit from an oil salesman is not always a welcome addition to the day.

Occasionally I have been slung out. My sales patter has barely reached its second sentence when I have been interrupted by an instruction to 'Clear off', followed by precise details of where my reluctant customer's land ends and just what he intends to do to me should I be discovered inside his boundaries.

These, fortunately, are isolated instances. When it does happen I very seldom go back to that place. I reason that I may have missed out on the man's trade, but he is probably paying much more than he needs to for his essential oil. Most of the farmers I visit are very sociable. It helps that I am able to communicate on their level, because I have always lived in the country and know enough of the workings of farms to talk sensibly about what their duties might be at any given time of year.

Without being immodest, they probably find me interesting, too. Some have no sporting interests beyond shooting or fishing – both of which take up part of my spare time – but I have been surprised by the number who are genuinely keen on cricket and are fascinated by any insight I can give them into the game.

Now and again this can lead to spending more time than planned with a single customer. On many more occasions than I have been thrown out of farms, I have been welcomed with coffee or whisky, maybe both, and sat down in an armchair for a full afternoon of chat. Most dangerous of all are the farmers who get out their home-made wine. I am a glutton for it, and each one tastes like lemonade . . . but without exception they have a kick like a donkey and I end up regretting it all.

My job is basically to find new customers, establish their regular order and then deal with any complaints on my regular visits every couple of months. I relish the challenge of increasing my list, and find that most new orders arise from social occasions, notably shooting. If I am involved in a shoot of eight guns, the chances are that around five will be farmers, one may be a haulage contractor and one a factory owner. They are all potential customers to me because they all need oil of some description. I certainly don't throw myself at their feet, but in the course of a day's shooting conversation will naturally get around to my winter job and, as often as not, someone will ask me to come round and see him.

Dick Burge has become a very good friend; indeed, he served on my benefit committee last year, and his own sporting leanings are a great help. He understands that I may be called upon to undertake an overseas tour, whether for England, as has happened several times during our relationship, or on a private trip. Never yet has he stood in my way. Even when I have been touring with England, I have tried to get into the office for a month and visit as many customers as possible – and most of them know my position now, too.

It is solid work, five days a week for six months of the

117

winter, but I am grateful for it. The great thing is that I never wake up on a Monday morning with that feeling of dread. I actually enjoy going to work, even if it is winter and cricket seems a remote notion.

11

The Greatest of my Time

Whether Dennis Lillee was a faster bowler than Harold Larwood,
or whether Greg Chappell was ever in the same class as Don
Bradman, are questions that can only adequately be answered by
someone substantially older than Fletcher. But his own career in
cricket has now entered its third decade and he can talk with
authority and decisiveness on the greatest of his time.

Collecting autographs and picture souvenirs of favourite
stars and famous matches is a popular pastime for most
small boys who like cricket. But, in this respect, I was an
unusual child. Although I loved the game, I never sought
a single autograph, because I saw no point in it. From a
very early age I always preferred playing to watching
cricket, and I am no different now. Watching for long
periods bores me, and even when waiting to bat, I will
seldom see a ball bowled unless the bowlers in action are
completely new to me.

I had no heroes as a boy, in any sport. My aim was
always to be as good as the cricketers of the day, but I
never idolized them. Playing village cricket so young
meant that I saw very little of the first-class game until
I was actually playing it, but I do remember a couple of
visits to Fenners, special days out because the visitors
were Surrey and Yorkshire respectively. Even for a lad
with such a total absence of stars in his eyes, there was
excitement in the prospect of seeing Peter May, for Surrey, and Yorkshire's great Len Hutton. These were probably the players whose scores I followed most closely in
my regular studies of the county game in the newspapers,

and I considered seeing Hutton make 50 was part of my education.

Once I started playing for a living, Essex took over my life. It was a world in itself for a teenager, and although I do not think of myself as having been particularly impressionable or fanciful, I naturally became intensely involved with the characters of the club. Trevor Bailey was past his best, but had clearly been an outstanding player, yet the first player I really admired was Barry Knight, a superb striker of all but the quickest bowling, and talented in every department of the game. Another, of the same generation, was Gordon Barker, a name which will now be barely remembered outside Essex, yet he was a player who had everything but the vital edge of ambition to take him to the top. When the ball was moving around, Gordon could look a masterful batsman, and I believe he had more ability than many who played for England, both in his time and since.

As my career progressed and broadened, there have been many cricketers who have impressed me, but none has approached the brilliance of Garfield Sobers. I don't believe there can ever have been a more complete player, and perhaps there never will be. But one of the most striking aspects of Sobers was the totally different ways in which he tackled a Test match and a county match.

He gave some fine performances for Notts, and gave them service I would not presume to denigrate, but I had the impression that the county game was never quite sufficient to demand his full attention. He enjoyed it, but took it rather less than seriously. In a Test situation he was a far more solemn and intense character, hardly smiling at all early in an innings and plainly giving every game his entire concentration. Sobers was easily the best batsman I ever saw, and I have vivid memories of his range of shots, all played with a minimum movement of his feet. To me, this is a mark of great players, who never lunge either forward or back in exaggerated fashion and seldom move their feet more than a few inches in either direction. Sobers had been brought up on good, quick wickets where confidence was instilled in him to hit through the ball from a balanced position.

As if his batting were not enough for any mortal to be blessed with, Sobers was also an outstanding new-ball bowler. His spin bowling was nothing special, and when he employed it at all it was generally a tactic to buy a wicket. But as a seamer he was extremely dangerous. I faced him a number of times in Tests, and can vouch that he not only moved the ball prodigious amounts in the air and off the pitch, but that he also did it at an unexpectedly lively pace from that silky smooth run-up. An incomparable cricketer.

Only two batsmen of my era can be talked of in the same breath as Sobers, and they are Greg Chappell and Barry Richards, both breathtaking strokeplayers when conditions are right, but capable of the most correct defence if the ball is moving or the pitch is bad. Viv Richards is obviously a superb attacking player and would certainly be in my top five, whereas the gutsiest players under onslaught from quick bowling are Geoff Boycott and Australia's Ian Redpath, whom I have seen survive some torrid hours and violent blows, still keen to stick it out and come back for more.

There have been plenty of top-class fast bowlers around over the past twenty years and, like any other truthful batsman, I cannot claim I have enjoyed facing any of them. But one stands out, comfortably clear of the field. Just as Sobers was untouchable as a batsman, Dennis Lillee is very plainly the finest pace bowler of my era, if not of any era.

Some bowlers of this type have pace in their favour but little else. Lillee, quite simply, has everything. He frequently bowls well within himself for four balls of an over, slipping in two exceptionally quick deliveries from an action which scarcely seems to deviate from normal. He does exactly what he wants with the ball, swinging it either way but bowling the outswinger – by some distance the most dangerous delivery for a batsman to face – with control and consistency. I played against Fred Trueman, late in his career in 1963, but he had not lost his speed

121

and I consider him very similar to Lillee, though without the final edge of command. Something they both had in abundance was hostility, the evil streak which hates every batsman who happens to find himself on the receiving end. Even in 1970, when Lillee was only 21 and just starting out in the game, he had plenty of devilment in him and no fast bowler can achieve real heights without that certain something in his temperament. If you are going to bowl fast, one of your main weapons is fear, intimidation, and you cannot produce that effect by being a nice bloke. Andy Roberts was another evil pace bowler – very straight, very fast and with the same wicked streak. John Snow had it, too, but since he retired it has been sadly lacking in the England team, only Bob Willis coming close.

Mike Procter had very little opportunity to prove himself on a Test stage, but I would still put him in the highest class as a fast bowler and very much more besides. In my view, he was the best overseas cricketer to come into the English game, because he gave so much to Gloucestershire, and to county cricket in general, by his wholehearted attitude. He was a formidable opponent but, somehow, it was always a pleasure to be involved in a match with him. 'Prock' was positive and committed in everything that he did, and if I had to pick someone to play for my life he would be very near the top of my list.

One hears plenty about West Indian and Australian fast bowlers, but for the past couple of years New Zealand have had one as good as any. Richard Hadlee was a fairly ordinary bowler when I first encountered him in Test cricket, but there is nothing ordinary about him now. He is skilful, hostile and frequently very fast, and I can give him no greater praise than to say he is very nearly in Lillee's category now.

But it is, of course, the black West Indians who have dominated the quick-bowling scene for some time through sheer weight of numbers. If Roberts is past his best, there is an ever-lengthening queue waiting to take over. In their current Test squad, Michael Holding, Colin Croft, Malcolm Marshall and Sylvester Clarke are all in the top bracket for pace. I put it down to the pitches on which they learn the game. Caribbean Test wickets may not be as fast as they used to be, but the club teams still play on bouncy, helpful wickets which encourage youngsters to run in and bowl as fast as possible. The process is perpetuated by the fact that their Test fast bowlers are the island heroes and the natural inclination of the lads is to try and imitate them.

The opposite applies in Pakistan, where Imran Khan must be just about the first genuinely fast bowler they have produced, and in India, famous only for spinners until the talented Kapil Dev came on the scene. Things may be changing now, but for years past these two countries prepared their pitches to suit slow bowling, and no youngster was encouraged to do anything different.

Bishen Bedi, the Indian Sikh, was the best spinner I ever faced in Test cricket. I specify Tests, because Bishen was never the same threat when he played for Northants. English county pitches tend to turn, often quite sharply on the final day, and Bedi bowled too slowly to fully exploit them. Derek Underwood was a far better bowler in England, and more than once Essex's Ray East outbowled Bedi on a turner in a county game; but put him on a typical Test wicket, which turns slowly and reluctantly, and Bedi's looping flight will always be effective as it gives the ball a chance to bite.

I mentioned Underwood, although I really don't think he can even be compared with Bedi. They may both be classified as left-arm spinners, but there the similarity ends. Derek was a great bowler, but essentially an English-style bowler, who could do a containing job at virtually medium-pace but who would attack with great effect on a pitch that helped him at all. He was, unfortunately, past his best by the time I led England to India in 1981, but at his peak he was the classic dual-purpose bowler. He gave nothing away at any time, and if conditions were in his favour he would bowl you out. No captain could ask for more than that.

If Bedi was the most consistently threatening of the great Indian spinners, Chandrasekhar was the most unpredictable, and consequently the most dangerous. For a so-called slow bowler he delivered the ball at extreme pace and his greatest weapon was exaggerated bounce. When England toured in 1972, he had added the ability to turn his leg-break appreciably, which he had seldom done previously, and with the modern trend for four or five men, at least, clustered around the bat, he could be an alarmingly difficult proposition, especially early in an innings.

I rated Prasanna a better off-spinner than Venkat, with whom he was frequently contesting a single place in the Indian Test team. Prasanna's most effective delivery was the one which drifted away from the right-hander and went straight on after pitching; his control was absolutely immaculate. Venkat was more like the West Indian Lance Gibbs who, despite his total of more than 300 wickets, never struck me as being in the very highest class of off-break bowlers. His enormously long fingers produced top-spin bounce which accounted for many of his victims, but much his greatest advantage was bowling behind Wes Hall, Charlie Griffith and Gary Sobers. Any batsman's eyes would light up at the sight of Gibbs after surviving a session from those three great quick bowlers. Prasanna was never in that fortunate position – India's new-ball bowlers were generally given a token couple of overs to get some of the shine off the ball before it was tossed to the spinners for the real cricket to begin. Australia's Ashley Mallett enjoyed similar benefits to Gibbs, coming on after Lillee and Jeff Thomson had done their worst, and although he was a very capable off-spinner, this often gave him unrealistically flattering figures.

Wicketkeeping is an area in which England have seldom been short of ability, and Alan Knott is in a class of his own, so far as I am concerned. Australians will make out a strong case for Rodney Marsh, who took plenty of justified criticism in his early years before improving dramatically. He was determined not to be considered second-rate and his dedication turned him into a most accomplished 'keeper, but I still don't believe he even approaches the ability of Knott. Alan is a complete natural but often misunderstood for his idiosyncrasies. For instance, on tours he would always be out of bed around 6 a.m. and then spend an hour or more in the bathroom cleaning his teeth and doing a routine of exercises. He had to be given a single room eventually, but he continued his singular ways and people came to realize it was simply his way of motivating himself. In my view he was the nearest thing to a genius behind the stumps and some way above four others I would rank roughly equal – Marsh, Bob Taylor, India's Farokh Engineer and Wasim Bari of Pakistan.

England used to excel at slip catching. Phil Sharpe and Peter Parfitt were both brilliant in that position during my early years in the game. Now, we have gone some years without having an outstanding slip, but general standards of outfielding have improved beyond recognition. When I started playing, anyone who so much as bent to make a stop was considered unusually good, but nowadays every side has at least one outstanding fielder and there are very few individuals who fall below acceptable levels.

Derek Randall, David Gower and Paul Parker probably stand out in England, but there are many more who would have been considered exceptional up to a few years ago. One-day cricket has hastened this improvement, making county sides practise fielding and catching far more than was ever thought necessary in the sixties. For my best all-round catcher, however, I look to Australia. During the seventies their close fielders were kept busily occupied as batsmen fended off Lillee and Thomson, and Ian Redpath and Ashley Mallett both became very safe catchers. None was quite in the class of Greg Chappell, though. I have seen him take blinding catches in various close positions, and in the deep. But I can't remember him dropping many.

It is always interesting to reflect on great cricketers, and dressing-room conversations will frequently turn into lively debates on the relative merits of certain players. Everyone has opinions about fellow cricketers and, even within the confines of one side, those opinions can vary

125

enormously, so it can be seen that the job of Test selectors is perhaps more complicated than some people appear to think.

Having played in fifty-nine Tests, over a period of fifteen years, I sat down to choose the best England team I could assemble. The qualifications were simply that I had to have played with or against them all, but they also had to fit into my idea of a balanced eleven. This was the outcome:

1. Geoff Boycott. If only he had been more dominating, more adventurous, he could have been among the greatest players of all time. As it is, I will remember him as the best technical, defensive batsman I have seen. Contrary to some opinions expressed, I consider him a very brave player against quick bowling – I particularly remember one searching spell bowled at him by Keith Boyce in 1973, which only a player of great courage could have survived. I just wish Geoff had relaxed a little sometimes, forgotten about breaking records and turned his mind to winning matches.

2. Graham Gooch. Cricket will forever be full of ifs and buts, but if only things had been different, this could have been a lasting and effective opening pair for England. Boycott's obduracy and Gooch's colourful aggression complemented each other and made them a very difficult pairing to oppose. I have naturally seen a great deal of Gooch through playing for the same county, and have no reservations about his ability to take on and destroy the best of bowlers on good pitches.

3. Ken Barrington. A cheerful and instructive mentor to so many young England players in the final years before his tragic death, Kenny had previously been virtually the perfect number three in his long Test career. Once or twice he found himself in trouble for scoring too slowly, but how we could have done with him in recent seasons! Kenny could play shots delightfully when the need arose and the mood took him, but his great strength was his solid defence, an absolute essential in this position.

4. Tom Graveney. Too often, Tom is spoken of as being

simply an 'elegant' player, which suggests he batted in a
loose fashion. He was far more than that. A front-foot
batsman with a cover-drive that certainly was elegant,
Graveney could also bat very soundly in adversity. His
weakness was probably good off-spin, which he never
quite seemed to master, but I am interested and encouraged to note that he became a better player late in his
career!

5. David Gower. It was tempting to choose Colin Cowdrey for this position, but in the interests of balance,
Gower seemed a better proposition. It is always useful for
a side, and irritating for opposition bowlers, to have a
left-hander in the middle-order and Gower plainly has
the ability to be a great player. He may not quite have
reached his peak yet, but there have been clear signs
recently that he has matured. He is also an exceptional
fielder, either close or at cover.

6. Ian Botham. I could hardly have chosen anyone else
for the all-rounder's position. Of others in this category
during my time, I rated Basil D'Oliveira very highly as
a batsman, and Tony Greig combined his fierce competitive spirit with the knack of producing match-winning
innings or bowling spells and the ability to catch almost
as well as Australia's Chappells. But Botham is now better than either of his predecessors with both bat and ball.
If he stays fit, I hesitate to imagine just what records he
may create.

7. Alan Knott. I know Bob Taylor has his supporters,
but Knotty would be my choice on pure wicketkeeping
ability alone. His batting, cheekily brilliant at its best, is
a great bonus at this point in the order. I hardly remember seeing Alan drop a catch in a Test match, and as we
played most of our Test cricket together, that covers a
considerable period.

8. Ray Illingworth. Mike Brearley is the best English
captain of recent times, but Ray would lead this side as
he runs Mike a good second and deserves a place as a
player. He was the best off-spinner I played with, even if
he did have a tendency to pick and choose his times for

coming on. When the chips were down he frequently produced a good spell, and was also no mug with the bat.

9. John Snow. The best English fast bowler I have seen, and surely one of the finest ever. At his quickest, in Australia under Illingworth, he was as fast as anything we have seen from the West Indians in recent years, and just as mean with it. A very great fast bowler who never found the partner with whom he could have made England such a force.

10. Bob Willis. Another 'if' . . . if only Snow and Willis could have bowled together regularly for England. They might have rivalled Trueman and Statham as an English partnership. Willis has overcome some bad injuries to his knees and come back to play his best cricket when well past the age of 30. In 1982 he was probably bowling quicker, and more intelligently, than ever before.

11. Derek Underwood. In modern Test cricket, with pitches covered, Derek is not quite the same threat he was. When the pitch was left open to the elements he was always a potential match-winner, unplayable on a wet wicket. His strength was his control, and it was much more the way that he disguised his changes of pace than the amount he turned the ball that got people out.

Someone else might choose a very different team from the same period. But these are the Englishmen I have most admired during my time in the game – and I think this team would take some beating.

12

Thinking Them Out

*Even now, eight years after the event, English cricket followers
talk frequently of the 1974–5 tour of Australia and the heavy defeat
imposed chiefly by Dennis Lillee and Jeff Thomson. Some hark
back with an air of reverence for two undeniably great performers;
others introduce a note of scepticism and tend to dismiss the efforts
of a number of English batsmen as an inability to counter quick
bowling. Fletcher is among those who have been forever tainted by
the reputation, and it still irritates him now. The issue, however,
is not merely one of batting ability but psychology, and it dovetails
with another subject close to Fletcher's heart – the thought processes
and memory banks which all good captains put to use.*

Denis Compton once averaged 9 in a series against
Australia, when Ray Lindwall led the opposition attack.
Compton was a better player than I could ever be, but
still he struggled dreadfully against a great fast bowler at
the peak of his career. That statistic is probably painful
for 'Compo' to recall, but I use it whenever I am confronted by the familiar accusation that I 'was never much
good against fast bowling'.

Frankly, there were times when I became heartily sick
of hearing how I, along with a number of other English
batsmen, had apparently been exposed as inadequate by
Lillee and Thomson. The claim is as unfair now as it
would have been if applied to Compton against Lindwall.
It is simply a fact of life that an outstanding pace bowler
will always take wickets, and that a good deal of them
will come cheap. Any side which happens to have two

great quick bowlers working in tandem is fortunate indeed, and that was the case in Australia in 1974.

Dennis Lillee has got good players out for more than a decade now, and although he has lost the edge of speed which made him such an awesome proposition, he remains the finest bowler I have ever faced. It is not only the English he has tortured; I remember Sunil Gavaskar, surely one of the best post-war openers, having a miserable time against him when India played a series in Australia recently, and more than one of the flashing strokeplayers of the West Indies have had similar troubles.

Whenever I faced him I was looking initially to play him from the back foot. Simple sense, really, because against an extremely quick bowler on bouncy pitches, you are putting more than your wicket at risk by lunging forward.

If he did pitch the ball right up, I could still adjust my first movement and come into the ball. If anything was wide of the stumps early in my innings, it would be left well alone, and on the good, hard pitches of Australia it was often possible to leave a ball pitched on off-stump if it was just short of a length, confident that it would pass harmlessly over the top. I recall seeing Bob Simpson and Ian Redpath, two fine players of the new ball, walking away from the line as soon as they saw a ball pitched short on off-stump – but they would never have got away with it, nor probably even attempted it, in England, where inconsistent bounce dictates you must play everything pitched on or close to off-stump.

Various tactics were devised against Lillee and Thomson. Fred Titmus's exaggerated shuffle across his stumps was one, and Tony Greig's angled-bat slash over slips against the rising ball was another. Greig, however, was really copying Doug Walters, who had used this shot against John Snow in 1970–71, quite successfully until Ray Illingworth stationed a third-man half-way to the fence and had Walters caught there twice.

Anything different is worth trying, because the warfare is as much psychological as physical. A bowler like Lillee will constantly be trying to unsettle the batsman, who in turn should be aiming not just for survival but for something which may confuse the bowler.

The bouncer is naturally the fiercest weapon of Lillee's pace, and the best bouncers are not those that sail highest over the batsman's head but those pitched in the batsman's half of the wicket and rising to throat or head height. Some will counter-attack with the hook, but these days, those who play the shot frequently will find two or three men stationed in catching positions on the leg-side. I find it best just to take avoiding action, and have seldom attempted a hook since very early in my career.

The fast bowler's armoury does not end with delivering the ball. Some, and Lillee in particular, add to the intimidation process by abusing the batsman verbally. In 1974 the Australian captain Ian Chappell was responsible for orchestrating this, and I think it was much worse on that tour than I have ever known it, either before or since. It was nothing new. In fact, it has long been considered a part of the game in Australia, but Lillee probably took it to unfortunate extremes, while his partner Thomson scarcely said a word to anyone while bowling.

'Sledging', while chiefly the province of fast bowlers and close fielders, is ultimately under the control of the fielding captain. Chappell encouraged it and, two years later, Tony Greig led a good deal of chatting by England players during the series in India. My own view is that it is wrong to talk to a batsman with the sole intention of putting him off, which is what it amounts to. I have very seldom done it as a captain, and I would not encourage any of my players to indulge.

A captain's job, nevertheless, is bound up with the aim of removing batsmen by any fair means at his disposal, and there is certainly some psychology involved in this. While I may not be an advocate of talking to batsmen, I am very much in favour of ignoring those who want to talk. This category includes many excessively nervy players, who find it eases their tension to have a conversation of small-talk with some of the opposition, or the umpire. Derek Randall is the prime example. Even after more than thirty Tests, and ten years in county cricket, he is jittery every time he comes out to bat, and longing to engage someone in conversation. He positively twitches early in his innings, but there is nothing to gain by helping him relax, so I instruct all my players to steer clear of him and let him prattle on to himself. There are others very nearly as bad on the county circuit, and similar tactics apply – ignore their attempts to talk and let them work themselves into an even more nervous state.

Many people seem surprised by the revelation that all capable captains have a store of information about opponents in their heads, and will act on it whenever a new batsman comes to the crease; but this is among the elementary essentials of the job. One has to know the strengths and weaknesses of individuals to act effectively against them, and the knowledge simply accumulates over the years until it is like a deposit account at a bank.

I never physically make notes about the habits of batsmen, and do not know of another captain who does. It is just a question of memorizing the way in which someone played when he made runs or, sometimes, the way someone bowled to a certain field or in certain conditions.

The process does not end on the field, either. I often think there is more learned about opposition players when chatting over drinks in the evening, or in a car on the way to games, than ever is learned during games themselves. The theory that cricket is a vocation rather than a job, and can only be played full-time by those who have a genuine love for the game, is borne out by the amount we all talk about it. I doubt whether there is another band of sportsmen, nor even another section of industry, who spend so much of their free time discussing their job. It may be boring for wives in the evenings, but there is no doubt it has its benefits. At Essex, I always encourage each of my players to contribute his own views and observations on the opposition, and after dissecting all I have been told, always find something of use.

My first priority when a new batsman comes in is to recall how best he likes to play and then attempt to block out all his favourite shots. The details of his strengths that

I have stored away in my brain come to the surface and I make the necessary adjustments to the field placings accordingly.

It may initially seem a negative move to defend against a player's strengths rather than to attack his weaknesses. But by frustrating his usually productive strokes, you are achieving a measure of attack by forcing him to look elsewhere for his runs and, hopefully, inducing some false shots.

There are times, of course, when you do the opposite and set a field designed to trap a player in the stroke at which he is most unhappy. Sunil Gavaskar, for example, is a wonderful player but there are three ways in which I always consider I have a chance of removing him. He occasionally dabbles with the hook shot, and plays it up rather than down. So I have one or two men behind and square on the leg-side. He also likes to use his wrists against the seamers and clip the ball in the air, very fine down the leg-side. So I station a leg-slip for the shot when he comes in. Finally, I believe he is far less happy against spin than seam and has a tendency to bat-pad the spinners to silly point, another position I will fill as soon as I have the chance to introduce a slow bowler.

Another who likes to hook is Derek Randall. The shot has got him out a number of times at international level, but he still plays it instinctively, so it is worth instructing my quickest bowler to let him have a few short balls, and set the appropriate deep fielders for the shot.

When discussing batsmen's weaknesses it is important not to allow the theories to become fanciful. The simpler the better, to my mind, and the major weakness of every batsman is the ball which pitches three inches outside off-stump and leaves the bat. It is too close to the stumps to leave, so the batsman is committed to playing a stroke. If bowlers could produce deliveries like that to order, a captain would seldom have to worry about complicated field settings – a few slips would be sufficient.

David Gower is one player often accused of being weak outside off-stump. Frankly, I do not accept that he is 'weak' anywhere, but he does play an apparently loose, semi-sliced shot to deliveries slanted across him. The ball often comes off very near the middle of the bat, but because he has his bat angled, it will fly in the region between slips and gully which is frequently untenanted. To capitalize on this, it is often a good attacking move to have someone at fourth or fifth slip for Gower, rather than first or second. His other risky shot is a clip off his legs, which usually means having someone at 45 degrees to the wicket, behind square. Of course, Gower may very well still make runs despite these moves, because he is a very good player, but you know you always have a chance in these two areas.

I tend to see more of Graham Gooch from the dressing-room or the non-striker's batting crease, as he is an Essex team-mate, but if I were faced with trying to get him out I would certainly have a backward square-leg, just behind the umpire. Goochie is a player of great power who uses an exceptionally heavy bat, so when he mistimes an on-drive and gets an inside edge, the ball will often fly for 4 through that unguarded area, where a fielder might just take a catch.

If Gower and Gooch are two of the three best stroke-playing English batsmen of recent times, the third is un-questionably Ian Botham. I have often watched in wonderment as he takes Test-class attacks apart but, while his eyes certainly light up when he sees a spinner come into the attack, I think he is more likely to get out against them than against a seamer. I certainly introduce a slow bowler as quickly as possible when he comes in against Essex, and ask Brian Hardie, our witty Scottish opener, to put on his helmet and go into the short-leg position.

Hardie, known to us all as 'Lager' for the obvious reason, is a very brave cricketer with the bat and in the field, and anyone standing close against Botham needs all the courage he can muster. There has recently been plenty of talk about prohibiting the use of helmets by fielders – a move I am set against. The bat-pad position is accept-able in the game, but it is undeniably dangerous, and I feel each side should be allowed one helmeted player, which would almost always be the short-leg. Botham is quite likely to hit a man on the head in that position, but he is also prone to popping up a catch against the spinner.

His other unconvincing shot is the sweep. Against Abdul Qadir of Pakistan last year he was often in trouble through top-edging a sweep, and at Lord's he fell to a catch on the boundary, backward of square-leg. With a spinner operating, I would always have a man there for Botham.

When I think of overseas strokeplayers in the county game, two of the most menacing are always Viv Richards and Zaheer Abbas, men who have raised the standard of their respective counties down in the west and done much to generate new interest in that part of England.

Richards is best tackled by a policy of containment. Not outright defence, which gives him easy ones and twos to get into his stride, but with a field of, say, two slips and two men in the mid-wicket area, where he so often chips the ball with power and great effect. Block off that shot and he may well lose patience. I used to set a very similar field to Rohan Kanhai, who very often picked up a lot of his early runs through mid-wicket.

Zaheer is formidably strong through the cover region, so anyone who bowls wide of off-stump is giving him easy runs. But he does play slightly across the line of anything straight, so a medium-pacer bowling a full length at middle stump has a chance against him. I have also noticed that he ceases being such a fluent batsman if the ball turns at all.

All this is just a sample of the theories and memories I can call on, as can most other captains on the circuit. The job may appear to the uninitiated to be merely a question of tossing a coin, roughing out a batting order and giving a few instructions in the field, but there is very much more science to cricket captaincy than is apparent from the boundary and beyond.

Bowling changes are by no means as rigidly planned as many people seem to imagine. It is not simply a case of giving the seamers the new ball, bringing on a medium-pacer as first change and then turning to the spinners. The conditions, the state of the game and the batsmen at the crease all have a large bearing on any bowling change, and experience is all-important in terms of timing it right.

The job is made much easier if every player is prepared to think about the game and chip in with suggestions. Unfortunately, no side has a full complement of thinkers and Essex are not unusual in having a couple of players who dream their way through a day in the field, often wandering out of position.

Motivating a team should hardly be necessary after a time; they are all professionals and should be aware enough of their responsibilities to realize what is needed. But a good captain senses which individuals in his side need special attention, whether it be a sympathetic word or a kick on the backside.

So much of the game, as I have said, revolves around psychology of one type or another, and if one thing is certain it is that captains should improve, like good wine, with the years.

13

Sacked – the Darkest Days

Keith Fletcher had returned from the arduous tour of India and Sri Lanka a beaten captain, but surely not a disgraced one. To lose the first Test of the Indian series had strategically been a disaster, the Indians being masters of containing cricket, but Fletcher's conviction that England were the stronger side throughout was borne out by most of the succeeding drawn matches. In Delhi, Calcutta and Madras, potentially powerful positions slipped away, and while some sections of the media were critical of Fletcher's leadership, both in terms of tactics and discipline, he has resolutely stood by his decisions and pointed out the hazards of umpiring, gamesmanship and pitches which had been given the equivalent of a sleeping draught.

When he flew home following victory in the inaugural Test on Sri Lankan soil, Fletcher confidently expected to keep the captaincy, if only for a part of the summer to come. If his confidence diminished in the weeks ahead it was through what was not said, rather than what was, and nothing had prepared him for the evening of Friday 21 May.

What do you say when a man on the end of a telephone line tells you he is taking away a treasured part of your life? Because that is precisely how I felt when Peter May rang me shortly after 4 p.m. on that May afternoon. It was the most shattering moment of my life.

Many people have experienced the distress that comes with being sacked from a job. But I would suggest the captaincy of England is rather more than just a job. It is an honour, the highest in the game to my mind, and after a number of years hoping I might attain it, and several more feeling certain it had passed me by, it is difficult to explain the extent of my emotions when I was appointed for the Indian tour. Privilege, certainly, and achievement, too, plus a sense of boyish excitement and a determination to hang on to it for as long as possible. I did not kid myself that I was being thought of as skipper for years to come – at 37 I was grateful for the belated chance. But I did expect to be given a fair run in the job. I was prepared to work tirelessly for England and show the selectors loyalty in return for their faith. But I found out on 21 May that they were not prepared to show me any faith.

Perhaps I should have been prepared for it. Maybe it should not have come as such a shock to me. But, although the longer the uncertainty went on the more little doubts crept into my mind, that phone call still hit me like a hurricane and left me literally speechless.

I admit that I returned from the tour in full anticipation that I would be continuing in the job. Presumptuous, maybe, but a captain newly appointed for a full tour does not normally expect to be ditched immediately afterwards unless one of two things apply: either that the tour has been a complete shambles, and despite the 1–0 defeat I don't think anyone could justifiably level that assertion at our Indian expedition; or that the captain has gone only as a stand-in and fully expects to hand back the reins at the end of it. Well, I had taken over from Mike Brearley simply because he was not available to tour – I have no doubt whatever that he would have been appointed if he had simply said the word – but he was not keen to make a third comeback to the job and had already announced that he would be retiring from the game at the end of the 1982 home season.

There appeared to be no other obvious candidate. Ian Botham had lost the position once and seemed unlikely to win it back just yet; the senior professional Bob Taylor had made his reluctance to lead any team quite plain with Derbyshire; and Geoffrey Boycott was counted out on three issues – his relationship with the players, his behaviour in India, and now his principal role in the tour to South Africa. Bob Willis, of course, had been vice-captain of the past four tours and had certainly been a wise and capable deputy to me. But fast bowlers have very seldom been thought tactically or temperamentally suitable for the captaincy and as Bob is the type who gets unusually wound up in the emotion of his own game, he was seldom mentioned as a serious candidate.

So, taking all these factors into consideration, I felt I was justified in my optimism. I assumed that I would have done my cause no harm by declining the offer to lead the English side in South Africa. I have already detailed just how tempting that was, but I played everything by the book. It was not so much a question of trying to make an overt show of loyalty; I simply felt it was a dishonourable thing for an England captain to involve himself in.

All appeared to be going to plan when I was made captain of the MCC side against the champion county, Notts. As this match is traditionally played in the first week of May, before a scattering of hardy souls at Lord's in weather requiring two or three sweaters and hot drinks instead of orange squash, it is not the most popular fixture on the cricket calendar. But leading MCC still carries a degree of prestige, and I was not even unduly worried when Mr May, as the new chairman of selectors, said that nothing should be read into my appointment or the MCC selection. I put that comment down to natural diplomacy and continued to look forward to renewing battle with Sunil Gavaskar and the Indians.

I was convinced, correctly as it transpired, that England would turn the tables and win their home series. My belief that we were the better side on tour was not, I know, unanimously shared, but in English conditions I knew things would be very different. There would be stronger umpiring for one thing, and far less tolerance shown to the blatant time-wasting which so frustrated us all in India. The prospect of beating the Indians, putting the record straight, certainly filled me with enthusiasm. There are times when I find it difficult to get into a season, when the early weeks in cold weather are anything but inviting. This year I had no such reservations, and as I had started off in good form with the bat, life looked rather good.

Sue was sharing my good times, just as she had been obliged to share the bad ones, the disappointments and the setbacks over the years. She had suffered enough of that and I know she was savouring my achievement as much as I was. Pretty soon, she was to know better than anyone just how much it had meant to me.

MCC played the Indian tourists at Lord's on 19 May, a three-day game which is often, these days, the closest we come to a Test trial. I was neither made captain nor selected in the team, but as it was a largely experimental side, with David Gower in charge, the decision certainly seemed far from terminal with regard to my future. David has matured rapidly, as a player and a personality, and I know plenty of administrators share my view that he will one day be captain of England. But he repeated regularly in public that he was keen to hang on to his freedom and independence a while longer and did not feel he was ready to take on such a major responsibility. The MCC game was plainly a good opportunity for the selectors to study him directing a side, but it did not seem likely that they were thinking seriously of asking him to take on the England job just yet.

What I could not understand, as the days dragged by, was that neither Peter May nor any of the other selectors had been in touch with me. I did not necessarily expect any verbal assurances, but I did assume it was customary for the chairman of selectors to consult with the captain of a recent tour, if only for some background to the games and some guidelines on individual players. Peter May had, of course, available to him my written report on the tour, but he had never been to India as a player and it was just not possible for him to have any conception of the singular difficulties posed for a visiting side – unless he asked. I wonder, even now, on whose information he was relying. Probably he spoke with Raman Subba Row, our fine manager and a colleague of May's at Surrey. But although Raman was in touch with the pattern and events of the tour, he had not been on the field. It seemed to me to be a strange way to go about picking a team.

I knew from the press — no other source — that the selectors had been together during the MCC-tourists game and learned from a friend on the Friday morning that an announcement about the captaincy was expected that afternoon. My first reaction was an almost resigned 'well, it can't be me, then'. But on reflection I decided that they had probably not finally made up their minds and that I was still in the favourite's position.

Essex had no game that day and I spent most of it in the garden. Events at Lord's were never far from my mind, though. The phone, on the wall in our kitchen, rang a number of times during the day, mostly people wanting to discuss benefit business and forthcoming functions. It was after 4 p.m. when I picked it up to hear Peter May's voice on the other end. Immediately, I thought this was it — he was just phoning to confirm that I would remain as captain, probably for the three Tests against India.

Instead, in his polite and measured tones, he just thanked me for what I had done in India and told me that the selectors had decided to make a change. The new captain was to be Bob Willis.

He wished me luck for the season, told me that he would be delighted if I made so many runs that they had to pick me again as a batsman. I am not sure if I actually gave a hollow laugh or whether it was subconscious, but I knew as well as he did that my England career was finished.

If I had scored 2000 runs by the end of June I don't think I would have won back a Test place. This, surely, was the end. For nine years I had wandered in and out of the Test side, never secure from one game to the next. When, in 1977, I came back from Australia after a depressing performance in the otherwise memorable Centenary Test at Melbourne, I had been prepared to accept I would not play again for England. When I was recalled as captain it was like a child receiving the best Christmas present a few weeks late, unexpected but delightful. Now, to continue the analogy, I had hardly got the wrappings off the parcel and it had been snatched away.

Peter May's phone call to me had been made just fifteen minutes before he announced the change to the press, and it was the first time he had spoken to me since the tour. The way I felt that night, if he had never spoken to me again I don't think I would have been too sorry.

Many thoughts had flashed through my mind while he was breaking the news to me. Many sentences were partly framed, and then left in limbo. I said nothing, just put the phone down. I felt terrible, drained and depressed as I had never felt previously. I did not need to tell Sue. She had been more worried about the decision than I had been in advance – maybe she feared the worst, as I should have done. Now, one look at my face told her all she needed to know. There was nothing she could say to console me and she was sensible enough not to try.

Unfortunately, young children can never be quite so tactful. My two girls did not understand what had happened, or if it got through to them at all they could not have been expected to realize what it meant to me. They remained as indomitably chatty as ever, and suddenly I knew I had to be alone. It may sound melodramatic, but that is exactly what I felt. It is very easy to philosophize, to say it solved nothing by being miserable, but just try smiling after being kicked in the stomach.

Captaining England on tour had been marvellous. I had relished every moment, even in defeat, and it had realized one great ambition. But to lead the side at home, on English soil and with an English crowd, that always seemed the ultimate to me. In the space of a few seconds on the phone I had been asked to accept that I would now never have the chance.

I left the house in a hurry and took off in my car. Where I was going, I neither knew nor cared. The objective was simply to get away on my own with my thoughts. They were bitter, malevolent thoughts, I confess. I believed I had been badly let down, and will always believe that they were wrong, if not in the decision they took, then in the way it was done. I had been open with them over the highly controversial South African issue and had turned down a small fortune, in cricketer's terms, because I wanted to keep the captaincy and keep faith with the men who gave it to me.

Hindsight might breed easy haste, but I am prepared to say I would have gone to South Africa, taken the breweries' money and captained the so-called 'rebel' side, if I had known what was in store for me. Why not? I was nearing the end of my county career, and if all hope of playing for England again had gone, only moral reasons could possibly stand in the way of earning available money from the game. I have already made it clear that when it comes to South Africa, my moral outlook is simply that every cricketer has the right to choose, and that no government should hypocritically interfere.

On that lonely, silent and confusing car ride, I tried hard to think of reasons for the decision, because none had been given. It would have made it a little easier to take if some sort of explanation had been forthcoming. I know Peter May was not obliged to give his reasons and as he had not seemed inclined to do so, there had been no point in me prolonging an agonizing phone call by asking him. But now I thought back through the Indian tour, wondering if it was my tactical handling of matches, my personal grip on the team or perhaps even my own behaviour which was being called to question. Peter May had stated publicly that he meant to make sure England's players respected a firm code of conduct on the field. Perhaps I had been sacked for knocking off that bail in Bangalore, all those months ago. Probably I would never be sure.

Much the most likely reason seemed to be the balance of the side. It suggested to me that the selectors had come to some conclusion about certain batsmen they wished to play against India, and that there was no room left for me. Certainly, when the Test side appeared, admittedly picked with Bob Willis's help, that impression seemed justified.

Allan Lamb was in, which no one in their right mind would debate. Our registration rules made him eligible and he was quite obviously one of the finest players to be seen in England for years. If it had come down to a straight choice between him and me as batsmen, I would quite rightly be the loser every time. But another name on the list was Derek Randall, a nervous, unpredictable player who shows flashes of absolute brilliance but can look very ordinary for much of the time. If I had been thrown out so that Randall could be given yet another in his saga of Test opportunities, it merely made my thoughts still blacker.

When I got home again, about an hour later, Sue told me that there had been a number of calls. Most of them were from the press and, although some of the callers were personal friends, I could not bring myself to discuss it with them just yet. But Bob Willis had also phoned, and I returned his call immediately. Whatever had happened to me was not his fault, and as we chatted on the phone it was clear that he felt confused; part of him was naturally delighted for himself, another part disappointed for me. We had been good friends for years and I hope nothing ever changes that. I wished him luck and meant it. If I could not captain the side which was to beat India, I was glad it was going to be the man known to us all as 'Goose'.

I took the phone off the hook for the rest of the evening. It was a long evening, too, and after a restless night I felt very little better. Saturday was a playing day, a Benson and Hedges Cup qualifier against Hampshire at Chelmsford, and when I walked into the dressing-room there was a solemn atmosphere the like of which I have very seldom experienced at Essex. They all showed sympathy, which was natural for a team-mate, but I sensed that John Lever and Graham Gooch were especially upset, having been with me through the problems of the Indian tour and then joined up with the party leaving for South Africa.

Somehow I had to try and put it all behind me and get back to county cricket. Essex had made a bad start to the season and my personal turmoil could not obliterate the need to put things right. Strangely enough, my sacking affected my form only in the sense of making me more determined. In the weeks which followed I made a pile of runs and felt I was batting better than I had done for eight or ten years. I was not deluding myself – I knew it would make no difference to Test selection – but at least if I had been ditched on the grounds that I was not a good enough player to command a place, it was satisfying to feel I was proving a point.

It took me a long while to come to terms with the episode well enough to even talk about it freely. I discussed it with the Essex players, of course, but not in any detail. For days which ran into weeks, I woke up every morning with a sense of loss, and I am not naturally a very emotional person.

Even in my darkest moments I never contemplated packing up the game completely, because I enjoy the life at Essex so much. But I have often had somewhat malicious thoughts about what I might do in the improbable event that England called on me again. In my imagination, more than once, I have accepted the invitation and then withdrawn on the eve of the Test, explaining that I would prefer to play for Essex.

None of the selectors has since discussed it at all with me. I have not seen nor spoken to Peter May again, and it seems ironic, now, to think that he was the player I most admired and looked up to when I was at school in Caldecote.

My future needed careful consideration. At the back of my mind I had thought that if things went well I might just have taken the team to Australia in the winter of 1982–3. When all such thoughts became fanciful, I had to adjust my plans, even to the point of deciding what I would do if I received a further offer to tour South Africa. Things would be different this time. I don't think I would turn them down again.

14

Where do We go from Here?

If Fletcher's England lot was not a happy one, he had the good fortune to be sustained by the atmosphere and the results achieved by his county. Essex may not quite have lived up to the rich, if belated promise of their two triumphs in 1979, but each succeeding year has had its share of success and the current side, stable for so long, has gained the respect of every other county. The years in which Fletcher's career was born, years when Essex was a cricket backwater and when challenging the game's giants seemed a remote dream, are long gone.

Like football fans who turn on their team after a few defeats, perhaps forgetting the good times only weeks earlier, some people in cricket have shockingly short memories. When Essex failed to win anything in 1980, I was astonished at the number of people within the club who began moaning that we had had a poor season when, in fact, we had reached the final of the Benson and Hedges Cup. Success can have a strange effect on people. Suddenly, the endless years of vain struggling are completely forgotten and anything but the best is thereafter deemed a failure. It is a blasé attitude which annoyed me at first, but thankfully it never extended to the Essex players. Their thirst for winning and their disappointment in defeat remains as strong as ever, but I am pleased to say they have sacrificed none of the humour and spirit which has characterized Essex teams in recent years.

I pity the many millions who claim they dread each new week of work. To me it is a pleasure, both during the summers of cricket and the winters with my job in oil. Only on very odd occasions have I lost my enthusiasm, and this has normally occurred in April, after a long winter tour with England. Then, just once or twice, I have felt stale, and unable to transmit the proper degree of motivation to others in the side. It has never lasted long, however, and once the fixtures have begun in earnest, I have always fallen happily back into a pattern which remains enjoyable to me even after twenty years of county cricket. I have never quite lost the sense of gratitude that I am being paid a wage for what is effectively an extension of my greatest hobby.

Nothing stands still, however, and sport has toughened its approach in much the same manner as business. People are generally far more concerned with winning than they were when I began playing. Part of it is the social development which dictates that success is all-important, but in cricket at least, the more professional attitude stems to a large degree from financial concerns.

The equation is one of simple logic, of course. Successful counties will attract more spectators, which brings in more money to be spread through the club, not least to the players. To me, it does not seem that long ago that the amateur players still held the dominant hand in English cricket, but in effect, it might as well be a century ago, such is the professionalism of the modern player.

Administration has not quite made a parallel advance. There has been progress, certainly, and there are certain top officials for whom I have the utmost respect. But still, on my travels around the country, I see a number of clubs which are not run on anything like the lines I would expect from what is undeniably a business concern.

The players' living depends, to a large extent, on the way their club is operated. Yet still there are too many people involved at the top level who are trying to run a cricket club after they have done a day's work elsewhere.

I accept there is not a limitless supply of money to finance salaries of officials, but I still maintain there is plenty of room for modernization. Essex, in common with a number of other counties, have a full-time chief executive in Peter Edwards, whose duties are less that of a secretary than, shall we say, a managing director in business. Most of the clerical work is taken off his hands by a secretarial team and Peter is responsible for the day-to-day smooth running of the club. It is a system which has worked well in recent years.

Another innovation has been the appointment of team managers by various counties. In places, they have been extremely successful, and I think especially of Surrey, where Mickey Stewart has confirmed my high opinion of him as a leader by moulding the players available into a winning unit and bringing success back to the Oval after a series of lean years. My view, however, is that the Surrey situation is an exceptional one, and in general I can see little value in the concept for county sides. Certainly, those who are strong and have an experienced captain, should have no need of a manager, whose main contribution may well be to diminish the authority of his skipper. This has always been my stance while captain of Essex, although I must say no one has even suggested to me that we should have a manager. I know Mike Brearley always felt the same way during his long and successful period as captain of Middlesex.

There are clearly some areas in which another supervisory figure can be useful to any club, however, and I cite Middlesex again as my example. While Brearley had full charge of the first team, former player Don Bennett had the title of manager, but spent almost all of his time with the second XI, coaching the youngsters and providing the link between the sides. If a vacancy occurred in the county team, Bennett was able to supply all relevant information about the form and attitude of those in contention. In the past two seasons, Mike Denness did a very similar job for Essex, combining his second-team duties with a promotional role.

One of the obvious questions I am very often asked is whether I will remain in the game in any capacity when I finally stop playing. It would be difficult, I think, to cut myself off completely. I have seen men do it, turning their back on the game that has been their life for so long, but

148

I don't believe I could, or that I would even want to make such a total break.

I can't see myself moving house to take a job with another county. My roots are in the Essex and Cambridgeshire region and I have no wish to desert them. So any future involvement in the game would have to be with Essex, and it is certainly my wish to continue with the club in some capacity.

Coaching has never appealed to me. I am afraid I have very little patience with children – my own sometimes included! – and supervising a class of twenty-five kids of whom only three really want to play cricket is not my idea of a fulfilling day. I have done some coaching over the years, of course, but never did take to it happily. General administration, and dealing with senior players, is much more in my line. I enjoy serving on various Essex committees and would like to continue that, even if my salary in future comes from outside the game.

I stress, however, that retirement is not yet part of my plans. In 1982 I felt I was batting as well as ever, still fielding adequately and certainly still enjoying the game, which is the key to it all. The day that I wake up thinking 'oh no, another day of county cricket' will be the day I plan to give up. As things stand, I hope I have another three or four years in the game with Essex, fitness allowing.

On a point of principle, I would certainly not have retired at the end of the 1982 season, even if I had felt like doing so. This was the year of my second benefit, reward for twenty years as a capped player with the county – and although the benefit is a distinction for past service, not an incentive for the future, I feel it is wrong to take the money and run. Retirement, following a benefit, is perhaps not as bad a sin as leaving to play for another county – something which has occurred more than once in recent years, notably when Barry Wood accepted a benefit cheque in excess of £60,000 at Lancashire and promptly joined Derbyshire, where he is now captain. This, to my mind, is a smack in the teeth for all the people who have supported the benefit. They give of their time, money, or both, because they appreciate the player's service to his particular county, and I doubt whether many of them would give so freely if they knew the player was only waiting for his cheque before seeking pastures new.

The benefit still works as a loyalty bonus and I would be sorry to see it abolished, as has been suggested in some quarters. It is all very well to claim that counties could arrange a stipulated payment to players who have completed ten seasons, but that extra money has to be found from somewhere. Although the absence of beneficiaries would open a number of fund-raising doors for the clubs themselves, it has been my experience that the public are more reluctant to contribute to a county than they are to an individual. Perhaps it is because they have no way of knowing to what purpose their money is being put when they donate to club funds; at least, when giving to a beneficiary, they are quite sure that it is the player who takes their money.

I also think there are good grounds for a supplementary benefit scheme to apply to players who may have started their career late, or changed counties for a good reason in mid-career, and just failed to complete the statutory ten years. We have had an example at Essex in wicket-keeper Neil Smith, a Yorkshireman who found he could not make progress in the game in his native county due to the opposition for places, so joined Essex in 1973. By 1982 he had been replaced as our first-team 'keeper by the younger David East and we released Neil at the end of the season, just as his benefit would ordinarily have become due. Players like him surely deserve some sort of reward to take with them from the game, and I know Essex did their best to help him financially.

The subject of player movement is always a contentious issue, and hardly a season goes past without someone suggesting that transfers between counties should be more freely available for dissatisfied players. I do not agree. As soon as cricket is allowed to adopt a soccer-style system of transfers, the game will be put back a couple of decades

150

to the time when two, maybe three counties dominated the Championship every year.

Free movement will inevitably lead to the rich counties becoming stronger and the poor, or smaller, counties losing their best players, and that would be disastrous for the competitive element which currently exists in the county game. In recent seasons Northants, Leicestershire, Somerset and my own club Essex have broken the monopoly of the traditionally successful counties such as Yorkshire and Surrey. Now, although there will always be two or three counties going through bad times, every competition is a far more level and interesting contest than would be the case if players were free to flit from club to club. For that reason alone I feel the Test and County Cricket Board are absolutely right to insist that each projected transfer is vetted and that a player must have an adequate reason for wanting to move.

Overseas players have also played a large part in creating a more competitive county circuit, which is why I am against the phasing-out process being conducted at the moment. I would agree that we were at one time allowing so many imports into our game that there was a very real danger they would soon outnumber English players, and that the position had to be adjusted. But we are surely going too far in restricting every county to only one foreign star. Gloucestershire, Northants and Somerset have all been inspired to winning trophies by their imports, and the success of counties such as these is good for the game.

I wonder whether Taunton would be quite such a vibrant, thriving place to play these days if Somerset had not been allowed to play Viv Richards and Joel Garner? I doubt it. The majority of foreign players of this high standard attract interest, new support and thereby money into the game.

The stipulation, I would suggest, should be nine Englishmen per county, which ensures that the matter is controlled while retaining the element of glamour that the likes of Richards, Procter, Lloyd and Hadlee give our cricket. I am set against the policy of registering as

151

English a player whom we realistically know will never play for England – Proctor being a prime example.

Yorkshire are perfectly entitled to their stringent policy which prohibits anyone even born outside the county, let alone the country, joining their staff. But while they may be admired for it, people should not forget that Yorkshire is an enormous county, a great catchment area for cricketers. So they should not have the thing both ways and continue to moan that they are not winning trophies because they have no foreign players. That was their choice, and no one forced them to stick by it.

There has recently been considerable debate on the future structure of the county game, a matter on which most players seem to have definite views. My own thoughts are that if the Championship were perhaps played over four days but certainly with each county playing all the others once only, this would at last create a proper competition, rather than the current lottery in which one title contender might have to play most of the weaker teams twice, while another has to play all the strong sides twice.

However, this is one cricketing improvement which should perhaps give way to commercial considerations. Counties like Essex and Kent, which attract tremendous local interest and sponsorship, would lose vast sums of money with the demise of their festival weeks, and all counties would surely lose members if all Championship cricket was played in midweek.

It has been fashionable for some players to knock the Sunday League, to claim that it is not really cricket and that county players should not be asked to 'demean' themselves by indulging in short slogging matches. I have never associated myself with any such complaints, because virtually since its inception I have found the John Player game to be superb entertainment for the players as well as the crowds. Nor do I accept that it is merely a slog. There is a very definite art to the 40-over game, one which in many ways tests a captain more than the traditional three-day cricket. Field placement and bowling changes become of urgent importance; get one wrong and the day can be lost. Similarly, one missed catch or misfield can be disastrous, so every county has worked hard to improve its standard in the field, and the difference over a ten-year period is quite extraordinary.

Winning the Sunday League is very nearly as difficult as winning the Schweppes Championship, and maintaining a lead in the competition is a hazardous business. Middlesex found that out in 1982, just as we at Essex had done some years previously. Middlesex made a marvellous start and looked as if they would at last win the competition for the first time. But they found that every one of the clubs near the foot of the table attacked their fixture against Middlesex as if it were their one big match of the year. They could not win the League themselves but they could at least have the satisfaction of beating the likely winners. As a result, Middlesex 'blew up' and found themselves overtaken by Sussex.

We had won the League in 1981 after finishing second more times than I cared to remember. But the following year, adopting what I thought were very similar tactics, we lost our first four matches. It was quite staggering, but it meant that we then had to win all our twelve remaining matches to have a realistic chance of holding on to the title. Impossible, everyone said. But we set about it in good, positive style and actually won seven in succession before losing our way. Our players go out on Sundays to enjoy themselves, just as I do, but we play each game hard and get a great deal of satisfaction out of the competition. I hope no one changes it so long as I am involved in cricket.

My next assertion in this essentially brief summary of the game today concerns the amount of Test matches being scheduled. The increase in the Test match programme over the past five years is remarkable, and has now reached unmanageable proportions; if too much is asked of players, the inevitable response will be one of declining performance, and I think this has already been noticeable in certain individuals. It is an obvious syndrome, but one the practitioners of Test planning do not seem to have realized. Even as great an international player as Ian Botham, to take an obvious example, cannot be expected to produce the same peak level of batting and bowling in twelve matches a year – and that is the number that top Test cricketers are now being asked to meet. Too many Tests will drain the players. The warning signs have been there for some years now, but it appears they have not been heeded. I hope somebody takes notice before it is too late.

It is undeniably true that most Test players do not give of their best in county cricket, and that the chief reason for this is that they have worked too hard for their country. Professional they may be, but no cricketer is a machine capable of turning out consistent performances day after day, no matter what the workload.

Test players are at least now being paid what they are worth. Funnily enough, it took Kerry Packer to bring the authorities to their senses. There are those in high places who will not thank me for reminding them of the fact, but Packer undoubtedly brought about the dramatic switch to professional thinking by our administrators; he created the opportunity for Cornhill to take up their mutually profitable sponsorship, and by indirect means I reckon he made the lot of the average county player considerably better.

I feel the current gulf is too great, however. Test players who take part in an entire twelve months of cricket can now earn up to £30,000 from cricket alone, never mind the endorsements, newspaper contracts and other promotional interests they attract. A county player is lucky if he clears £10,000 per year. That is too big a gap and I feel the county cricketer's rewards should be boosted from some source. I can already hear the familiar plea that the game is too poor to indulge in a further round of wage rises, but I would counter that by pointing out that a great deal of money was found extremely quickly by the authorities after Packer had completed his coup. Cornhill's cash came too late to save that revolution, but it would not surprise me if there was another unless steps are taken to bring the county player's salary nearer that of their immediate superiors.

The only men to have made substantial amounts of money from the game are those who have played Test cricket regularly since 1977, the year when Packer's plans were hatched. I was never against World Series Cricket, nor those who joined up, but just like those who went to South Africa five years later, they ought to have known the consequences of their actions and not feigned or claimed surprise when they were subsequently banned. It was sad, in the case of Packer's project, that it was staged in direct competition to official Test cricket. But maybe there was no other way; certainly it has improved the financial standards of most players.

If Packer and South Africa have been among the great cricket talking points of the past five years, then umpiring has undoubtedly been another. It certainly seems almost an inevitability in each Test series these days that the visitors will object to the umpiring, and I am not at all certain that most of the claims are unjustified.

The natural tendency for a squad away from home is to think they are being victimized by biased umpires. Very often they might be wrong, but standards have not been high recently, and in certain countries I feel they have been deplorable.

I would agree wholeheartedly that the pressure on the modern Test umpire is surely greater than ever before. The stakes are higher, and the intent of the players is plainly more aggressive. There is a lot more appealing than went on when I started playing, particularly for close catches in the recently invented bat-pad positions. The players constantly press the umpires, and sometimes, I suppose, they must crack.

The Australians are still the worst offenders in the field of verbal abuse, as they have always been in my experience, but both England and Pakistan would appear to be close behind.

An international panel of Test umpires, with neutral officials appointed for each series, might well be worth a try. It would probably not improve standards, but it could reduce the accusations of bias.

The game of cricket is probably as popular now as it

has ever been. Purists will flinch at that, and point out that full-house crowds use to pack the grounds for important County Championship matches; but I would contend that was before the days of blanket radio and television coverage, and before the days of one-day cricket. When the menu is tempting enough, the public will still support us. At other times, I sense there is still an enormous audience following every move of a season through the columns of the newspapers and the wavebands of the radio. Ten years ago people were trying to tell me cricket was dead. Nobody would dare now, and I would bet that it will still be vibrantly successful long past the time I hang up my boots.